Britain's Last Invasion

Britain's Last Invasion
The Battle of Fishguard, 1797

Phil Carradice

PEN & SWORD
HISTORY

AN IMPRINT OF PEN & SWORD BOOKS LTD.
YORKSHIRE - PHILADELPHIA

First published in Great Britain in 2019 by
Pen and Sword History
An imprint of
Pen & Sword Books Ltd
Yorkshire - Philadelphia

Hardback ISBN 9781526743268
Paperback ISBN 9781526765857

Typeset in INDIA By IMPEC e Solutions

Printed and bound in UK by TJ International Ltd.

Pen & Sword Books Ltd incorporates the Imprints of Pen & Sword Books
Archaeology, Atlas, Aviation, Battleground, Discovery, Family History, History,
Maritime, Military, Naval, Politics, Railways, Select, Transport, True Crime,
Fiction, Frontline Books, Leo Cooper, Praetorian Press, Seaforth Publishing,
Wharncliffe and White Owl.

For a complete list of Pen & Sword titles please contact

PEN & SWORD BOOKS LIMITED
47 Church Street, Barnsley, South Yorkshire, S70 2AS, England
E-mail: enquiries@pen-and-sword.co.uk
Website: www.pen-and-sword.co.uk

or

PEN AND SWORD BOOKS
1950 Lawrence Rd, Havertown, PA 19083, USA
E-mail: Uspen-and-sword@casematepublishers.com
Website: www.penandswordbooks.com

Contents

Foreward

Ifirst wrote and published an account of the 1797 French landings at Fishguard more years ago than I care to remember. It was a slim enough volume and it has now been out of print for some time. The original publishers, Village Publishing of Pontypool, stopped producing books just after the end of the twentieth century and the beginning of the twenty-first. Since then hardly a month has gone by without someone ringing me up and asking if I have any spare copies to give away or sell. And if not, why do I not reprint?

Without wishing to get into a debate with my concerned callers about the differences between writers and publishers, I have always noted their interest and promised to do something about it at some stage in the future. This is it.

One thing is certain. There certainly seems to be a continuing interest in the subject – and that, really, is what this new book is all about, the enduring fascination with a little known but highly relevant and significant event. Time to put money – the publisher's money, I hasten to add – where my mouth is!

It would have been very easy to simply produce a new printing of the original book but, like most writers I guess, I have an in-built antipathy towards much of my previous work, particularly books that have done well – as this one undoubtedly managed to do.

So although it would have been considerably easier to reprint the original version, I decided I would prefer a new book, one that would be based on the first 'Last Invasion' – if you see what I mean – but which was written in a somewhat different style and incorporating new material and facts that have since come to light. In that way, I hope, the book will be fresh and will capture old readers as well as new ones.

It is over 200 years now since the French Legion Noire landed at Fishguard. That was the last time any invader's foot has ever trodden on the fields and hills of mainland Britain – if you take out the occasional First World War U-Boat crew landing to replenish water supplies or rogue parachutists and fifth columnists descending on the Home Counties during the second great conflict of the twentieth century.

Certainly this was the last attempt to achieve dominance on something more than an individual basis – in this case 1,400 bodies more than an individual basis. Whether that dominance was an attempt at invasion remains another matter.

The Last Invasion, if that's what it was, remains a fascinating story; one of lost opportunities, missed chances and effects that were unknown and unrealised at the time but which still resonate here in the twenty-first century. It is a story that deserves to be told, again and again. I hope that readers, old and new, agree with that assessment and immerse themselves in the stories of General Tate, Barry St Leger, Lord Cawdor, Jemima Nicholas and the rest. There is only one way to find out – read the book and let me know.

Phil Carradice, St Athan, February 2018

Introduction

Ask any casual passer-by or workmate in the canteen, any fellow drinker in the pub or passenger on the commuter train, for the date of the last invasion of Britain and they will probably respond with 1066. Clever ones might give you the answer 'The Channel Islands in 1940', so you will have to re-phrase the question – 'Mainland Britain, I mean mainland Britain. When was the last time mainland Britain was ever invaded?'

Mostly you will still get 1066. Possibly, just possibly, the answer will be 1688 when King James II, the last Catholic monarch of England, fled the country to be replaced by William of Orange and his wife Mary in what has always been known as the Bloodless Revolution.

Both answers would be wrong. The last invasion of mainland Britain actually took place on a mild February evening in the year 1797 when a 1,400 strong French legion landed on the Pencaer Peninsula outside Fishguard in Pembrokeshire.

The French landed unopposed and there, on the rugged coast of West Wales, they established a tenuous beachhead. It was three days before the invading forces were rounded up and herded into captivity – but what a three days they were!

The invasion was a foolhardy affair – not that it was ever intended to be. But as they unravelled, the threads and events of those February days turned out to be farcical. It was soon clear that they had more in common with the *Carry On* series of comedy films than they ever did with the bloody and vengeful campaigns of the French Revolutionary Wars.

Sadly for the French but intriguingly for us, the invasion was doomed to failure almost before it began. It was part of a more detailed, but just as hopeless, series of adventures and military campaigns; campaigns that culminated in the last military unit to attempt an invasion of Britain coming ashore in Pembrokeshire. After those few confused and contradictory days of mania and lethargy, the episode was over, consigned to folk lore and to memory.

The 'What if?' school of history has never been a particularly rewarding way of proceeding, but if any event ever demanded the question it has to be the French landing of 1797. So let's get them out of the way early on.

Above all there is the issue of what might have happened if the Directory, the ruling council of Revolutionary France, had followed up this sudden and totally unexpected success by reinforcing and extending the beachhead? There was little to stop them and the results might just have been world shattering.

There are several dozen more questions that could, and arguably should, be posed. What if the invading army, known by the dramatic and panic-inducing name of the Legion Noire, had been first-rate troops of the line rather than the desperate and degenerate group of cutthroats who, in reality, made up the invading force?

What if the commanders of the Legion Noire had been leaders of quality and determination rather than the lacklustre and self-interested men they really were?

There are so many 'What ifs'. So many, in fact, that the student of history or the general reader is assailed by images of the destruction that might have been wrought, not just in Pembrokeshire and Wales, but in the whole island of Great Britain. If just one or two of those 'What ifs' had been able to step out of the realms of fantasy and become reality, the world would now be very different. Perhaps that is why the story of the invasion remains such a fascinating and compelling one.

The year 1797 was significant in British history, some of the happenings great and some of them small. And all too often it is the minor event that is most interesting, most fascinating. Put simply, we can learn from minor as well as from major moments in our past.

In the grander scheme of things the naval mutinies at Spithead and the Nore paralysed the Royal Navy for a short time and left the country wide open to disaster. By some miracle – and it was a miracle, as smugglers who regularly exchanged goods with their counterparts across the Channel kept a firm jaw and a closed mouth about the goings on – the French did not realise the opportunity they had been given. It was a short-lived window, one that was effectively closed by the way the British authorities dealt with the mutineers and their demands.

It was the year that Nelson, still then a little known naval officer, lost his arm at the siege of Santa Cruz on Tenerife. He apparently returned to his ship, arm mutilated, and climbed on board unaided. Then he simply turned to the ship's Surgeon and told him to get his instruments ready.[1]

1797 was also the year that the writer Jane Austen saw the spa city of Bath for the first time. Despite the popularity of the place and despite what she was later to write about it she hated the city and all it stood for. When, a few years later, she was told that her family was going to move there to live she did the only thing that well brought-up ladies of the time could do when presented with unwelcome news – she fainted.[2]

Above all, of course, 1797 was a time of invasion scare and fear of French domination. The last invasion of Britain is now only a distant memory. Even at the time it was soon forgotten, overshadowed by greater and more world-shattering events. And yet it had repercussions that went far beyond any impact it should have warranted. Several of those repercussions remain with us today.

And it is not only that. The stories that emerged from the landing, the invasion if you want to call it that, are the stuff of legend. They are tales that not even a novelist could have invented. That is what makes the story so interesting.

A Brief Note on Illustrations and Images

So many of the participants in the events of February 1797 have not been commemorated or remembered visually. There are, for example, no known portraits of Colonel William Tate, Jemima Nicholas, Lieutenant Colonel Knox or any of the Irish officers who served with the Legion Noire.

Many of the minor characters who appeared, briefly, then vanished from the story remain mere cyphers. They intrigue partly because of their vagueness, leaving the historian and the reader with no idea what people like Lieutenant Dobbin, William Fortune, Colonel Colby and Thomas Nesbit actually looked like. Were they tall, commanding, handsome or nondescript? At this distance in time those are questions that cannot be answered.

The lack of any image of William Tate is probably the most frustrating aspect of the story. Apart from anything else, a portrait, or even a sketch, would have laid to bed, once and for all, the debate about his age. Perhaps at some stage in the future someone may uncover an image but it is unlikely. If there had been a portrait it would have been found by now.

Just commissioning a painting of yourself was, in the eighteenth and nineteenth centuries, an expensive business, not like modern photography. It is unlikely that William Tate, always living beyond his means, would ever have had the money – or, for that matter, the ego – to pay anyone to record his likeness. Tate will probably remain as elusive to future writers as he has been to those of the past. It is part of the mystique and charm of the event.

Fortunately there are images available which depict some of the places that are a crucial part of the story – views of the landing, impressions of the surrender, and drawings of houses and generic views of the town of Fishguard. There are also portraits of some of the more significant players, people like Lord Cawdor, General Hoche, Robespierre and Wolfe Tone.

Obviously, visual depictions are not always essential. Images formed or created by words are often far more useful and significant. But every little bit – in picture and in words – helps bring alive an event like the last invasion of mainland Britain. They fill in the blanks and help create an understanding of the times and of the environment. Enjoy the images, enjoy the text.

Chapter 1

A Prelude to Disaster

Tregwynt House, five miles west of Fishguard, mid-afternoon on 22 February 22 1797:

The light was already fading when Mrs Harries' guests filed into the low-beamed dining room of her elegant and welcoming country house. The room was warm but it was filled with a thick, acrid smoke that seeped into the corners and the curtains, even into the wallpaper, and made everyone, ladies and gentlemen alike, cough delicately into their sleeves or kerchiefs.

The servants had recently laid and lit a fire in the wide grate at the far end of the room but it was not really needed; the day had been mild, surprisingly mild for the time of year. Mrs Harries, however, was not taking chances. Once the sun went down it would probably turn colder. They would have to put up with the smoke, Mrs Harries told herself, wet wood would burn as well as dry, once it got going, and everyone would be grateful for it later.

The guests had just settled themselves down at the dining room table when the sound of horse's hooves clattering on the cobbles of the courtyard outside brought all of them to their feet in alarm. All day there had been rumours of French ships off the Pembrokeshire coast, of soldiers landing and houses burned, women left bloody and lifeless in the hedgerows.

One of the guests had come armed with the story, happy to chill everyone to the bone with the images of what he had supposedly seen.

Nobody took it into his head to contradict him. The conversation for the past hour had been about nothing else.[1]

It was mid-afternoon, the custom of the times demanding that full use was made of daylight while it still lasted. Winter evenings were long and gloomy. Good quality candles were expensive, and it was common enough for houses in this part of the world to be shuttered up and bolted for the night by eight or nine o'clock. So, to be sitting down to dinner at four in the afternoon was, therefore, not out of the ordinary.[2]

Besides, Mrs Harries' dinner was to be followed by a dance. To have called it a ball would have been to grace the occasion with a grandeur it really did not warrant. Tregwynt was only a country house, a large country house it must be admitted, and one with a renowned sprung dance floor that ladies and aficionados from all over the county talked about with envy. But it was still just a country house.

Balls were for the nobility and gentry of the county, the Lords Cawdor and Milford, and their ladies. Mrs Harries, the widow of Captain George Harries, was not wealthy enough to afford a full scale ball, much as she might have liked the idea. No, it was to be a dance, a charming and delightful way to end the evening in this, the very dead of winter.

That, at least, was the plan. The messenger now hammering frantically at the front door might have put a different slant on things. The scuffling of footsteps and the mumble of muted voices from the hallway did not ease the anxiety that was now creeping like a winter frost across the room.

While alarmed guests were still debating the identity of the new arrival, the dining room door burst open. There, panting and red faced, stood a private in the local defence force, the Fishguard Fencibles. All heads swung around to the far side of the table. There, Lieutenant Colonel Thomas Knox, commanding officer of the Fencibles, was standing magnificently erect and glaring at the messenger.

'Well?' he demanded. 'Stand up straight man! What the Devil is the meaning of this?'

The Private swallowed and tried to pull himself erect. He failed dismally, jogging from foot to foot in his excitement.

'It's the French, sir,' he finally managed to gasp. 'The French, they're here.'

In staccato bursts he passed on the news. It was a tale that was as simple as it was stunning. French warships had moored off Careg Wastad Point on the Pencaer Peninsula, just a short distance north of Fishguard, a bare four miles from where they now stood. It appeared as if the troops on their decks were preparing to disembark.

For the dinner party guests alarm was immediately superseded by panic. One woman sobbed, another swooned into her chair and several of the gentlemen tried hard to pack the bowls of their pipes or reach into their snuff boxes without their hands shaking too much. Only Thomas Knox remained, on the outside at least, calm and in control of his emotions.

Britain had been at war with Revolutionary France for four years and the threat of invasion was strong. News of an abortive attack on Ireland only the year before was still filtering through the tortuous communication channels of the time. So, now, to find the French here at Fishguard, under their very noses – the prospect was terrifying.

'I am afraid I must go,' Knox said, taking the hand of a visibly displeased Mrs Harries. 'Stay calm, all will be well.'

'If you must,' the hostess muttered. 'Though what I will do with the mutton chops I really do not know.'

Knox strode out through the doorway, the messenger following meekly in his wake. Knox knew that his place now was in Fishguard, at the head of his part-time troops. For the next few hours the safety of the town, even of the whole country rested on his young and inexperienced shoulders.

* * *

With hindsight, it is impossible not to view the events of that February afternoon in 1797 without shades of the greater conflict of Waterloo – then, still eighteen years in the future – intruding into the picture.

In 1815, on the eve of Waterloo, the Duke of Wellington would be attending the Duchess of Richmond's ball in Brussels. That was where the news of Napoleon's swift advance into Belgium, a move that took all of the Allied strategists by surprise, first reached him via the hands of another mud-splattered messenger. The duke would react swiftly in the face of what he immediately perceived as terrible danger.

Knox, in 1797, might have been at the more prosaic dinner party and dance of Mrs Harries but the message was just as urgent and the danger just as great. And to begin with at least, he acted just as swiftly and just as correctly as the duke.

As soon as Knox left Tregwynt for Fishguard, Mrs Harries' remaining guests scattered like leaves before the winter wind. Carriages and horses were hastily summoned, those who could not wait left on foot. Within half an hour they had all gone.

Once back in their houses most people gathered together their most treasured possessions and valuables and fled south towards Haverfordwest or Narberth, anywhere as long as it was well away from the coast and from the marauding Frenchmen.[3]

Only one of Mrs Harries' guests kept his head and at least some vestige of his dignity – an old soldier by the name of Colonel Daniel Vaughan. Armed with sporting guns and pistols, he dismissed his servants and barricaded himself into his house at Jordanston. There he waited, almost eagerly, for the French to attack. Luckily for him – and, probably, for the French as well – the attack never came.

Not many of the local gentry were as determined as Daniel Vaughan. In most of the other large country houses around Fishguard, panic ran rife as news of the invasion spread. Like the guests at Mrs Harries' dinner party, all too many of the wealthy people from the town and area fled south. They were lucky. They had the time, the wealth and the means to effect an escape into the interior of the county. For the majority of the people in and around Fishguard – farm workers, shop keepers, fishermen and sailors – there was no alternative but to sit it out and see what materialised.

In the hours and days ahead it was to be these people, ordinary working men and women who were, in reality, little better off or higher on the social scale than the peasants of rural Russia, who were to be the decisive factor in the campaign. It was not a deliberate act – at least, not until Lord Cawdor took a hand – but rather an example of stoic acceptance and an inbuilt dislike of anybody telling them what they should do.

As with so many wars of liberation, the reaction of the ordinary people was to be crucial. Forget Thomas Knox, Lord Cawdor and the rest. They might plan and scheme, play at being soldiers, but it was the ordinary common people of Pembrokeshire who would ring the death knell for the invaders.

Like the land on which they lived, the farming people of North Pembrokeshire were rugged and solid, rarely given to hysteria and overreaction. Fishguard was a port, a town with strong connections to the sea and the men and women who earned their living from that sea were equally as hardy and just as used to privation and adversity as their farming colleagues.

While farmers and sailors alike might shake their heads and wonder why the French had come to their remote corner of the country – even today a region with few strategic or tactical advantages – they were never going to be panicked into hasty, unnecessary and ill-timed reactions.

They were, quite simply, not the types to run away. Damn the French, let them come; they would not scatter like rabbits before the scythes of the corn cutters and harvesters. Not that they had anywhere to run to.

Their lives were set in Fishguard and the surrounding countryside; they had no rich relatives who would take them in until the trouble had passed. No, they would stay and see what happened. They had bent before the wind of the conquerors many times and would undoubtedly now do it all again.

The landed gentry and the better-off gentlemen farmers were different. They were much more inclined to run away, as many of them did.

To start with they had considerably more to lose. Their wealthy and elegant lifestyles – or at least their wealthy and easier lifestyles – had given them status. The Revolution in France had already seen landowners, property magnates and the newly rich, people just like them, dispossessed, robbed and wheeled out to face the guillotine in squares and boulevards across the nation. It had been a bloodletting of epic proportions and it had happened just twenty miles away across the English Channel. They had no desire for something similar to happen to them.[4]

Everyone knew the French were rascals who would rampage and steal anything they could get their hands on. They had done it in their own country, now they had come to do the same thing here. The local gentry were, frankly, terrified.

Their fine collections of porcelain, their books, and their jewellery – it was all there for the taking. They were, these mini-squires and would-be aristocrats, these masters and mistresses of all they surveyed – at least in their somewhat pompous and inflated opinions of themselves – the perfect targets for looting, murder and mayhem.

Many of these people were incomers to the area and, as such, remained rather aloof from the men and women who had farmed the land or fished the rivers and estuaries for many years. As Commander E.H. Stuart-Jones has said: 'They were comparative newcomers to Pembrokeshire, and were not looked upon too favourably.'[5]

And so, in the main, they ran. It was left to the farmers and the labourers, the shopkeepers and the shoemakers, the shipbuilders and the fishermen, the people who toiled day in, day out in this windswept and barren corner of the world to stay and resist the invader – to stay and, if possible, defeat him.

In the early moments of the invasion, however, it looked as if defeat, when it came, would come to the British, not the French. And to understand why it did not, we need to go back and look closely at the germination of the plan – the plan that was to culminate in the last ever invasion of mainland Britain.

Chapter 2

Revolution in France

The French Revolution, that explosive wave of popular but enormously destructive power that was to consume France and affect the whole of Europe for over twenty years, erupted in 1789 with the fall of the Bastille Prison on 14 July. That dynamic beginning was the apogee, the most significant moment in the reign of Louis XVI, but for several years the unfortunate king had been ruling a country that was increasingly discontented and disintegrating at the seams.

Louis' accession to the French throne in 1774 may well have been marked by 'a fanfare of archaic celebration' but it was not long before the absolutist power of the monarchy and government began to drain away. The causes of the revolution were many and complex, dating back to the times long before Louis became king. It would have needed a very great and able monarch to keep the seeds of rebellion from growing and flowering into life – and Louis XVI was neither great nor able.

Louis himself was able to recall only two occasions when kingship actually made him happy – his coronation and then, incongruously perhaps, when in 1786 he journeyed to Cherbourg to visit the newly created port facilities.[1]

Louis's reign was an unhappy time, not just for the king but for all of France. There were many watersheds, notably the recalling of the Estates General and the Tennis Court Oath of June 1789. It was the fall of the Bastille, however, on 14 July 1789 that symbolised the smashing away of the old order, the 'ancien regime.' The destruction of the Bastille and the freeing of the political prisoners that were held within its forbidding walls was an event of monumental importance and yet for some – for one man in particular – it was something that passed almost unnoticed.

In his diary entry for the day Louis recorded just one word – 'Rien.' Nothing might well have been the impression that 14 July left with the king but it does seem a strange message to leave to posterity. There is a school of thought that Louis's entry related, not to the events of the day but to the bag in that day's hunt. Either way, for France and for the French people the destruction of the Bastille marked nothing short of a new beginning.

Over the next seven or eight years a very different France began to emerge. Like any newly created regime it was hardly a smooth process. To begin with control and governmental guidance still rested in the hands of the upper classes, the men who had created the revolution in the first place. It is surprising to realise that the French Revolution was not, initially, a working class upheaval and that the demand for change came, not from the sans culottes, the Parisian poor, or even the middle classes but from people of influence within the ruling system.

The traditional image of French aristocracy, the be-wigged and jewelled fops much loved by Hollywood, is not technically correct. Many aristocrats were newly elevated to their titles and a large number of them had their economic security vested not in inherited wealth but in trade. These were the class of people who wanted political power to add to their economic and social value base. The king and the ancien regime were holding them back; it was as simple as that.

The first significant and powerful figure in the new chain of command was not the middle class lawyer or rabble rouser you might expect but an aristocrat. He was Marie-Joseph Paul Yves Gilbert du Motier, better known as the Marquis de Lafayette, hero of the American War of Independence. Lafayette was, above all, a restraining influence on the wilder elements in the new government and while he retained control in France, the body and the position of the king – if not his influence or power – were at least secure.

It was a strange situation. The king had been removed from government but he still lived and was still, officially, the monarch of France even though all his power had been taken from him. It was, at best, a stop gap situation and one that could not continue for very long. That was what Lafayette understood only too well. In the early days of the revolution he did his best to steer his monarch through what was becoming, on a daily basis, a minefield of ever greater proportions. The arrogance and self-delusion of the king did not help Lafayette in his task.

Elected to the Estates General in 1789, Lafayette also became the Commander in Chief of the National Guard. He tried to run a middle course but he was in the minority and in 1792 he found himself out on a limb, his views ignored and his position marginalised. When the inevitable warrant was issued for his arrest Lafayette fled to the Netherlands but was captured by Austrian troops and spent five years in jail. It might have been a fall from power that, in its own way, was as degrading as the king's but at least he kept his head!

Lafayette's problem had lain in the fact that, as with the fall of any absolutist regime, once people had tasted a little independence and power, they were not likely to stop short of demanding a great deal more. It remains a truism but in most revolutions the first upheaval is often accompanied by a second or even a third as the architects of the revolution almost invariably find themselves consumed by the flames of the vortex they have created. And that is exactly what happened in France in the 1780s and 90s.

Before too long, control of the country was no longer the preserve of the aristocrats like the Marquis de Lafayette but was resting, perhaps inelegantly and somewhat insecurely, in the lap of a political party or group known as the Girondins.

The Girondins took their name from the Department of Gironde in the south west of the country, a region that was home to many of the most important men in this collection of revolutionary thinkers. These were the individuals who now found themselves at the centre of the new French government. Their leader was the writer and pamphleteer Jacques-Pierre Brissot.

A loose-knit republican faction, the Girondins were part of the Jacobin Movement. The Jacobin Club – so called because of the old Convent of the Jacobins in the Rue Saint-Honore where they originally met – was to become the most radical of all the revolutionary groups from this period. They were the people who drove the revolution forward, a dynamic and brutal group of individuals.

To begin with, however, it was the Girondin faction from within the Jacobins that took the lead. The Girondins under Brissot were adamant that the monarchy must be abolished but, even so, they did not wish to kill Louis. The spiralling violence of the revolution and the increasingly radical nature of Jacobin ideals – not least the desire to execute Louis as a traitor – appalled them.[2]

Despite being something of a 'war party' with Brissot demanding armed conflict with the nations in Europe, for no other reason than to spread the revolution, clashes between the Girondins and the ever more radical Jacobins were inevitable. Just as it did with Lafayette, by December 1792 control was beginning to slip out of their grasp as the more vocal and violent Jacobins began to assume centre stage. With influential journalists and orators like Jean-Paul Marat advocating an end to Girondin control, further bloodshed was inevitable.

Republican France was, at this time, a whirlpool of confusion and disorder. Anyone with aristocratic leanings or connections had become vulnerable. It did not matter who you were or what use you had been to the regime in the past, the Republic was no respecter of reputations.

Marat himself was killed, stabbed by a Girondin sympathiser Charlotte Corday while he was bathing. Marat was obliged to resort to hot water almost every day to help cure a painful skin disease but he invariably eased his conscience by working while he was soaking in his bath. Charlotte Corday did not attempt to flee after killing Marat but stood there awaiting officials. She was arrested and executed four days later. Marat's murder was the subject of a famous and dramatic painting by Jacques Louis David, an artistic creation that admirably caught the mood of the time.

The Jacobins were now flexing their muscles and it was not long before Jacques-Pierre Brissot was taken into custody. Along with twenty-eight other Girondins, he was sent to the guillotine in October 1793 and the Jacobins – and all of France – slipped easily into what was to become known as the Reign of Terror. Bolstered by the power of the Committee of Public Safety, the sinister figure of Maximillian Robespierre now began to assume centre stage.

If there is one word to describe the period between the fall of the Bastille and the rise of Napoleon Bonaparte in 1799 it is confusion. And yet that single word hardly begins to show just how dramatic and terrifying those ten years really were. The old regime might have gone, but however autocratic it had been, the reign of Louis and his minions had, at least, been familiar.

Now constitution after constitution, governing clique after governing clique, each succeeded and supplanted the other in brutality and what, at times, seemed sheer stupidity. It was all done with frightening rapidity. And it was not only the government that was subject to rapid and repeated change. Even the army was affected, as Lucy de la Tour du Pin was to write:

> It was during the first few months of 1790 that the demagogues set out to corrupt the army. Every day some disturbing piece of news reached us: one regiment had seized its funds; another had refused to change garrison; in one place the officers had emigrated; in another a town sent a deputation to the Assembly asking for the transfer of the regiment stationed there on the grounds that the officers were aristocrats and did not fraternise with the citizens.[3]

Lucy de la Tour du Pin was an amazing character who wrote a fascinating account of these troubled times. Given her background and breeding she might have been expected to take a firm line with the revolutionaries. An intimate friend of Marie Antoinette and Talleyrand, among others, she was an aristocrat and a confidante of the royal family.

Lucy was actually with Marie Antoinette in her bedroom when the mob broke into the Palace of Versailles in 1789 and witnessed their depredations at first hand. By some miracle she managed to escape the guillotine and fled to America where she and her husband lived for many years as farmers. She returned to France at the beginning of Napoleon Bonaparte's reign as Emperor.

Her book, 'Memoirs of Madame de la Tour du Pin,' is surprisingly moderate but it does give a fairly accurate picture of the times. At the very least, her words provide some idea of the frightening degree of change and of the general degree of turmoil existing in France after the fall of the king.

Maximillian Robespierre, the new leader of the Assembly and, for a while at least, the most important person in the French government, was a lawyer and radical thinker. He was known as 'the Incorruptible.' Unlike Brissot and the Girondins he believed that the only way to ensure the safety of the people – and by that he meant the safety of the revolution – was by the instigation of 'The Terror' which would wipe out all opposition and, in particular, those who wished to undermine the new Republic. That Reign of Terror would eventually include the death of the king.

* * *

The French Revolution was greeted with shrieks of horror from many European nations and monarchies, particularly those having a joint border with France. In Britain, however, isolated and immune across the English Channel, there was much support and admiration for the uprising.

Radicals like Tom Paine, Richard Price and William Jones greeted the revolution with unbridled enthusiasm, viewing it as the logical extension of Britain's Bloodless Revolution of 1688 and of America's Declaration of Independence. It was, said Price, a glorious moment for liberty with despotism at long last being laid low in the dust.[4]

The poet William Wordsworth, perhaps understandably given his profession and the romantic, lyrical nature of his verse, greeted the event with a rather more flamboyant touch:

Bliss was it in that dawn to be alive,

But to be young was very heaven.

The Prelude 1805, Book X1[5]

In 1790 Wordsworth undertook a walking tour, from Calais to the Alps and this gave him the opportunity to see at first hand the effects of the French Revolution. There was, in his description of what he had encountered, a feeling of sheer realism:

> – – – A glorious time,
>
> A happy time that was; triumphant looks
>
> Were then the common language of all eyes;
>
> As if awakened from sleep, the Nations hailed
>
> Their great expectancy.
>
> *The Prelude* Book VI[6]

Enthusiasm for the revolution within Britain stopped short of government circles and the monarchy, however. The view of the Tory government was that people ought to know their place. The supreme example of men and women who did not know that place and who had failed to help maintain the status quo was available for all to see on the other side of the Straits of Dover.

Those who expressed their joy at the events in France were dangerous men and were soon highly suspect. Wordsworth and writer friends like Samuel Taylor Coleridge were, in fact, so enthusiastic in their support for the revolution that, for many months, they found themselves followed around and spied on by British government agents.

Tom Paine's seminal work *The Rights of Man* came out in 1792. It declared that every man (not every woman, it should be noted) must have the right to decide his future rather than accept society's rigid lines of demarcation. Paine also now found himself derided and under observation by the government.

He was aware of the furore his book had caused and knew that his freedom hung by a very tenuous thread. His only chance was to run for cover and the logical destination was Republican France. The British government tried him in absentia, Paine having sailed for the continent just twenty minutes ahead of the warrant for his arrest. When he arrived in Paris he was received with open arms, granted French citizenship by the new Republic and elected to the National Assembly.

And then events in Paris took a sudden and dramatic turn. For some time Robespierre had been forewarning the country about the fickle nature of the king and when, in the summer of 1791, Louis and his family attempted to escape from France it seemed that the Jacobins had been proved right.

Louis' Flight to Varennes was a drastic attempt at finding freedom. It was a desperate and, in many respects, almost romantic gesture – and it very nearly succeeded. The flight remains the stuff of poetry and drama – closed carriages, bodies cloaked by travelling blankets, horses straining at the leash and the clash of accoutrements in the air.

In the end, however, the royal family was apprehended before they could cross the border but to Robespierre and the rest of the Jacobins in the Assembly it simply proved that the king had placed all his hopes of survival on the ability to create military intervention by foreign powers. That meant he was no longer just a nuisance; now he was a liability.

The National Convention, effectively the second revolutionary government of France, was created on 20 September 1792. It came into existence with one major agenda, the ending of the monarchy and the life of the king. It's time in power was short as the Convention was effectively stripped of its powers by Robespierre's Committee of Public Safety in April of the following year. The Convention struggled on, however, a relatively toothless body but one that had achieved its main aim.

The monarchy was abolished almost as soon as the Convention succeeded the Assembly and Louis, who had spent the last few weeks of his life addressed as Citizen Louis Capet, was placed on trial and found guilty of treason. He was duly sentenced to death, going to the guillotine on 21 January 1793.

The execution of Louis in the Place de la Revolution in Paris was an act of regicide that caused utter consternation in the capitals of Europe. Deposing the king was one thing; killing him was a completely different matter and like the other major European powers, Britain found herself embroiled in the bitter and costly Revolutionary War.

Like most wars of the time, for the majority of people in Britain the conflict with France did not really touch them. The concept of 'total war' which is now so familiar to modern generations did not exist in an island country like Britain. Internal peace – apart from brief incursions like the rebellion of the Duke of Monmouth and the 1745 Jacobite adventure of Bonnie Prince Charlie – had reigned, more or less, since the Civil War.

There were consequences as far as trade was concerned but, by and large, tea, coffee and other beverages were still available in the coffee shops of Fleet Street. Bread was still produced and animals still went to market. Life went on more or less as normal.

Jane Austen is often accused of ignoring the long war with France which began soon after the execution of Louis XVI and lasted until Napoleon's defeat in 1815. But Austen, in novels like *Pride and Prejudice*, *Emma* and *Persuasion* was attempting to portray middle-class life at this time and, quite simply, the war did not intrude into the daily life of people like her fictional creations. Nowhere is this better seen than in her masterpiece *Pride and Prejudice* and the lives of the Bennett family.

For the younger Bennett girls there was no thought of death and disaster. But there was a sudden interest in the Regiment of handsome soldiers who had arrived unexpectedly in the tiny country town where the family lived. For the girls it was a culture shock. This was an attitude and a way of living that Jane Austen knew well and, like all good writers, she wrote about what she knew.

Yes, the towns were full of soldiers in flamboyant uniforms; and yes, there were militia men at country balls and warships moored in the Channel ports – all of which Jane Austen did actually write about. But the war, the battles and the bodies, the blood and fury of it all – they were something which happened far away on foreign fields and were the preserve of professional armies. It was not something that concerned young ladies whose only interest in soldiers was finding partners at the next dance.

The whole of the British Army numbered barely 45,000 men and of these, only 15,000 were available for use in the early campaigns against France. The rest were stationed across the world, protecting British colonial possessions.[7]

The French, naturally enough, took a different stance. To begin with they were fighting in defence of their revolution and their recently acquired freedom. They were powered by an ideal. Secondly, their huge reserves of manpower – 25 million as opposed to Britain's 7 million – ensured that while they might be lacking in tactics and training, their conscript armies had spirit and pride. They could be used as human battering rams against the thin lines of Allied troops.

The generals of Austria, Prussia and Britain had been conditioned in traditional military values, not far removed from the condotierri of Renaissance Italy – an army was a valuable resource, something to be harboured and preserved. Marching and manoeuvring were the key elements of any fighting force and so they had no answer to the French tactics.

Based on sheer weight of numbers, the famous French column attack – something that lasted as a tactic until Waterloo – quickly swept all before it. Besieged and surrounded by their enemies, expected to crumble before the weight of professional soldiers, the French amazed the world and smashed back the Allied armies on all fronts.

There were, obviously, setbacks and it was not all victory after victory. But within the space of a few years the Austrians and Prussians had been pushed back into the east, Spain and Holland had been forced to sue for peace and British forces under the Duke of York (now best remembered for the nursery rhyme rather than his limited military abilities) chased unceremoniously out of the Low Countries. William Pitt's first coalition was destroyed and soon Britain, protected by her surrounding oceans, stood virtually alone against the newly discovered might of Republican France.[8]

Britain and France had, for many years, been traditional enemies and now the leaders of the new French Republic saw Britain as the main proponent of the forces lined against them. In the eyes of Robespierre and his comrades Britain was the fermenter of counter revolution and was dedicated to bringing down the new Republic. In many respects they were quite right.

The British had had their civil war over a hundred years before and the constitutional style of monarchy that had been implemented suited their personality. Apart from the young radicals, Paine and Wordsworth and the rest, the Tory government – and it was, largely, a Tory government in these years – saw what was happening in France as an anathema.

So when in 1793 the Vendee and Brittany erupted into open rebellion against the Republic, it was British money and British weapons that lay behind what soon became a running sore in the side of France. If they were looking for a scapegoat, the Republic's new government felt, the burned out towns and the thousands of maimed or dead Frenchmen could be attributed to Britain.

The British inspired attack by émigrés and royalist supporters at Quiberon in 1795 was costly for both sides. It ended in disaster for the invaders and victory for the Republic. Just as important as the victory, it saw 70,000 muskets, many barrels of rum, thousands of blankets and hundreds of uniforms – British muskets, rum, blankets and uniforms – fall into French hands. It was proof positive, if any was needed, of the virulent nature of the British war machine.[9]

There was no doubt that the excesses of the Jacobins had seriously damaged the ideology of the revolution in the eyes of Wordsworth, Coleridge and the rest. Their hopes and dreams of a 'brave new world' had been shattered and, bitterly, they came to see that the new regime was, in many respects, no better than the old one.

In 1797, the year of the French invasion plans for Wales, Wordsworth and Coleridge decided they had had enough. They had been spied on, their walks – usually at night when they carried lanterns and notebooks – reported to the authorities by the locals. At the time they were living in Somerset, just across the Bristol Channel from where the French were to come ashore in Wales. It was not a deserted rural idyll like the Lake District; Bristol, then the second city of the United Kingdom, lay just a few miles away and the smoke of the copper and iron works across the Channel reached into the air like giant grey fingers.

Wordsworth's servants reported, at one stage, that they had overheard the poets talking about a 'Spy Noza'. In fact they were discussing the philosopher Spinoza and his work. Add all of that into massive disillusion with the course of the French Revolution and there is little wonder that Wordsworth and Coleridge quit the country and set off for a supposedly relaxing and rejuvenating tour of Germany.[10] They were not alone in their change of attitude.

Welsh radicals like David Williams retired in despair from public life as the activities of the Committee for Public Safety began to take effect. Tom Paine, highly critical of what he saw as a disastrous change of direction, was actually imprisoned in a French dungeon and only a stroke of sheer good fortune saved him from the guillotine.

On an intellectual level – although they would never have used such a phrase – the war had not been particularly popular in Britain, many believing that it had been misguided, others falling into the malaise of sheer apathy. The London mob, always to be relied upon to reflect the mood of the nation, had greeted the king on his journey to open Parliament in October 1795 with the cry of 'Bread, no war, no Pitt!'

Such words were ignored by Prime Minister William Pitt, who treated them with the contempt he felt they deserved. They may have garnered a brief nod of approval from Whig politicians like Charles James Fox but that was about all. In France, however, they were certainly heard and, more significantly, acted upon.

The Jacobins had fallen from power at the end of 1794. Robespierre had already gone earlier in the year. There were many reasons for his fall from grace but he had, it was felt, exceeded his brief and a warrant for his arrest was issued in July.

He managed to escape that first attempt to take him into custody but was rearrested when the National Guard stormed the house where he and a number of Jacobins were sheltering. During the melee Robespierre received a gunshot wound that shattered his lower jaw, but whether this was self-inflicted – several of his Jacobin comrades did manage to commit suicide – or whether it came from one of the attackers is not clear.

Robespierre went to the guillotine on 28 July 1794. To the end he was a controversial figure, beloved by some, hated by others, the type of figure who spans history but remains for ever on the edges of understanding and knowledge.

Robespierre and the Jacobins were, arguably, a means to an end. They had completed the country's masochistic need for self-flagellation and once the immediate external threat to the Republic died away, so too did the desire to look for traitors and victims within the regime. At that point they became expendable.

Our view of Robespierre has been skewed by the picture drawn by Baroness Orczy and her books. When we think of Citizen Robespierre we tend to think of the evil nemesis of the Scarlet Pimpernel – and, of course, the image that immediately comes to mind is from the extravagant and wildly inaccurate Hollywood films.

However, there is no doubt that Robespierre provided much-needed security for Republican France at a time when the country was in dire need of stability. Whether or not that security could have been provided in a less brutal manner is another question.

It is difficult to know exactly how many people were killed during Robespierre's Terror. One estimate puts the number of those condemned to death – not necessarily executed – at about 17,000. These were men, women and children who had been tried and convicted across France between the autumn of 1793 and July the following year. The executions were relentless and even on Christmas Day 1793 some 247 were guillotined. Many more died in prison while awaiting their date with Madame Guillotine.[11] The lucky ones were those who managed to remain alive, by oversight or by sheer accident of good timing, when the Jacobin Terror ended.

The fall of the Jacobins was followed by a further period of uncertainty before the Convention relinquished control of the country to the Directory which was created in October 1795.

With the coming of the Directory a new constitution was written and control of the country was passed on to a five-man clique which was to rule France until the coup d'état of Napoleon Bonaparte in 1799.

Perhaps the Directory's most significant achievement was the ending of the almost continual shedding of blood that had accompanied the Jacobin period in power. The Jacobin Club was closed and many of its members exiled from public life – many but not all. Enough remained to cause problems for the more conservative leaders of the new government, a problem that remained obvious for the four years of the Directory rule.

Chapter 3

The Directory Lays its Plans

The five-man Directory, along with its Parliament of two chambers, its advisors and officials, may not have been the most energetic or robust of ruling bodies, but they rarely had the money to do more than stumble from one crisis to the next. After the depredations of The Terror and the sheer horror of not knowing where the axe might next fall, the Directory can be perhaps excused for its somewhat lackadaisical approach to governing the country.

The economic crisis in France was serious. It was not helped by Britain's Royal Navy which kept up a continual and highly effective blockade of the French trading outposts across the globe and of the French coast itself.

Quite apart from that, after the bloodletting of the Terror and the rule of the Jacobins, France was ready for a more laid-back approach to government and world affairs, at least for a while – if, of course, the British would allow such a situation to take hold. There was no possibility of peace but the members of the Directory certainly hoped for an easing of tension.

The one Directory member of true genius was Lazarre Carnot, an engineer who had overseen many of the Republic's early victories. He was hampered, however, by the inbuilt conservatism of the other members of the Directory and by the fact that many of those now serving the state were more concerned about filling their own pockets than they ever were about the fate of the nation.

Carnot operated as President of the Directory and, as a student of military tactics and affairs, took particular responsibility for the reorganisation of the army. He created a system where two battalions of conscripts or volunteers served with each battalion of regular soldiers, something that quickly helped the new recruits become efficient and effective soldiers.[1] That was not his only achievement. In line with the ideals of the revolution, promotion in the army was now open to men of all classes, regardless of their birth. The emphasis was on ability, not social standing.

Under Carnot's leadership the revolt in the Vendee was finally crushed and, at last, the Republic had the breathing space to consider a final reckoning with that most implacable enemy of France – Britain. As far as Carnot and the other members of the Directory were concerned there could be only one solution. Britain must be destroyed.

One of the greatest weaknesses of any ideological revolution has to be the evangelical nature of the revolt itself. Revolutionaries rarely remain local – they expect others to subscribe to their beliefs and usually take steps to ensure that those who do not toe the line are forcibly converted. You can come with us peacefully or at the point of the sword, they seem to say, but you will come with us! The examples are obvious – Trotsky and his desire for worldwide communism; the twenty-first century terror groups like ISIS and the Taliban; and, of course, Republican France.

What fanatical revolutionaries the world over tend to forget is the almost equally ferocious denial of those they wish to convert. Those who are about to be converted, at the receiving end of the fanaticism, know that defeat will be fatal and therefore they resist to the bitter end.

Once the initial danger to the Republic had passed it was this innate desire to export their revolution that kept the idea of defeating and, eventually, invading Britain at the forefront of the minds of French military strategists. Even the French people, tired of external war and internal strife, saw that they would never find true peace until Britain had been defeated.

By 1795 Britain was isolated and at bay, all of the powers that had so eagerly declared war on France after the execution of Louis having found that the Republic was not such an easy nut to crack as they had first imagined. After the first four years of the Revolutionary War the British people realised that they and they alone, were now resisting the French.

It was a total about-face from the early days of the revolution when it had been Republican France that had felt hounded and hunted. The shoe was, metaphorically speaking, now on the other foot.

Unfortunately for the British there were also dangers a lot closer to home. The Society of United Irishmen had been formed with the intention of obtaining fair representation for Irishmen and Catholics, both in the Irish Parliament and in society at large. To begin with it was all low key and very politically correct.

Then came the realisation that, no matter what soothing words they might use, the British government would never yield to constitutional pressure. This realisation was quickly followed by awareness among the United Irishmen that if they wanted to obtain even the most limited degree of independence then they would have to take up arms to achieve it.

As a result, in 1796 one of the foremost members of the Society arrived in France in an attempt to enlist aid and support from the new French Republic. His name was Theobald Wolfe Tone.

Tone was an Irishman of French Protestant descent. He had studied law at Trinity College, Dublin, where he became enamoured with the idea of Irish independence. He obtained his degree and became a barrister. His real role in life, however, lay not within the law but was rooted in the vital and compelling business of Irish independence. It was not long before his activities were noted by government agents.

In 1795 Tone fled to the USA but he quickly discovered that he was not fond of the Americans, coming to view them as autocratic, reactionary and as self-opinionated as the British. He dismissed George Washington as 'a high flying aristocrat'. Realising that he had no hope of support in that direction he returned to Europe as an envoy to France.[2]

Assuming the name Citizen Smith, Tone had little understanding of the French language and no real contacts in the French capital. Always fond of fine food and wine, he enjoyed the restaurants of Paris – many of which had recently availed themselves of the services of the grand chefs of the ancien regime. But he was not just a pleasure seeker and he stuck gamely to his task, lobbying officials, writing letters and trying to convince the Directory of the benefits they might enjoy by helping the United Irishmen in their fight.

By now the idea of 'fair representation' had gone and nothing short of full independence was the aim of Tone and his companions. It was a remarkable shift within the space of half a dozen years but it had undoubtedly come about due to the intractability of Britain's Tory government. Wolfe Tone himself was to write that the aim of the United Irishmen was now to:

> Subvert the tyranny of our execrable government, to break the connection with England, the never-failing source of all our political evils, and to assert the independence of my country.[3]

Tone was conscious that, as an Irishman, he was still a citizen of Britain. If he should fall into British hands then the likelihood was that he would be tried and executed for treason. He therefore managed to persuade the French to award him a commission in their army. He was made 'chef de brigade', or colonel, although, at this time, he had no brigade or unit to command.

Then on 12 July 1796 Tone met the most important soldier in the Republic, the 28-year-old General Louis Lazarre Hoche. It was to be a crucial meeting, one that would take Tone back to his native shore and begin the process that would eventually lead to the landings at Fishguard.

Hoche was born at Versailles on 24 June 1768 and joined the Gardes Francaises in 1784. The son of a groom in the royal stables, Hoche was too lowly born to gain a commission, but he was efficient and capable enough to gain promotion to the position of non-commissioned officer. As such he was the man who commanded the National Guard when the angry mob stormed the Palace of Versailles on 5 October 1789. It was only his prompt action that saved the life of the queen, Marie Antoinette, putting his troops in their path when the rampaging mob had the scent of blood in their nostrils.[4]

It was perhaps strange that the man who would rise to become one of the foremost generals in the Republican army should have been instrumental in saving the life of the queen, the hated symbol of all that the ancien regime stood for and represented. At this early stage of the revolution, however, the mob was out of control and the last remnants of the aristocratic faction were still attempting to take charge. Hoche, while certainly not an aristocrat, was a serving soldier and, at that stage, was still one of their representatives with a duty towards the royal family. In the face of the revolution it was a stance that could not last.

Now fighting for the Republic, Hoche won fame during the siege of Dunkirk, an event that saw the British pushed out of Europe – not the last time that the town would serve as an evacuation port for a fleeing British Army. Further success and glory came during the Quiberon affair when Hoche was in the van guard of the main attacks on the émigré forces. In the wake of that victory Hoche was quickly promoted to the rank of general.

He was, for several months, imprisoned for treason during the Terror, having been denounced by one of his contemporaries. It was something of an occupational hazard at this time when all manner of people could level criticism or denounce anybody as a traitor to the Republic. Many such victims went to the guillotine but Hoche was lucky. He kicked his heels in prison and was released from captivity when the Jacobins fell from power. By the time he and Tone met in 1796 the young soldier was once again in a position of strength and importance.

Now the commander of three armies Hoche, like Tone, was possessed of a burning hatred of Britain and all that she stood for. He had witnessed the effects of British money and skulduggery at first hand, both at Dunkirk and, more significantly, at Quiberon. It was time, he felt, to do something about this viper at the throat of France.

Two other important members of the Society of United Irishmen were on the Continent at this time. Lord Edward Fitzgerald and Arthur O'Connor, both fanatical Irish patriots, were attempting to gain French help but neither had been particularly successful. The Directory refused to allow Fitzgerald to even come to Paris as he was too well known and the spies of William Pitt were everywhere.

If Fitzgerald was to be recognised and his presence in Paris reported back to Pitt there was no doubt that the Directory's plan would miscarry and nothing should be allowed to get in the way of that plan – for there was, now, a plan. There was to be an expedition that, hopefully, would cause maximum discomfort to Britain and, if possible, free Ireland from the yoke of British tyranny.

Arthur O'Connor, less well known than Fitzgerald, did actually travel from Switzerland to Rennes where he met up with General Hoche and there, together, they discussed the forthcoming expedition. Both Fitzgerald and O'Connor were significant players in the demand for Irish independence but their influence this time was negligible. Stuart Jones has written:

> The decision to invade Ireland had been made by the Directory on the day which Fitzgerald and O'Connor reached Basle, and two months before the latter met Hoche. It seems, therefore, that Wolfe Tone in Paris, by his persistence, his forcefulness of appeal … played the greater part in bringing the Directory to the point of launching an expedition which would, they hoped, detach Ireland from England and pave the way for the invasion of England herself.[5]

The plan was not one of Carnot's better ideas and was, in many respects, something of a madcap scheme. Its aim was very simple – it was, as Stuart Jones has said, to 'detach Ireland from England'. Once this was achieved England – and for England in all papers and letters of the time, read Britain – England would be finished. She would become a second-rate power. Such rather fanciful rationalisation could only have come from Tone and his fellow patriots.

Despite the fine words of the United Irishmen, Ireland provided little in the way of benefits for the British economy. It was a poor country where subsistence farming was the main way of life. There was little or no industry, no coal mining, no iron working and the like. The Industrial Revolution was gathering pace but at that time such developments remained largely the preserve of Wales, Lancashire and the North Country.

If Ireland did give something of value to the 'mother country' it was in terms of manpower. Hundreds of young Irishmen, despairing of making a living off the land, were serving in the British Army and navy. Tone put the figure in excess of 80,000 in the navy alone – but he was always prone to exaggeration and he did have a vested interest in stretching the bounds of plausibility.[6]

Initially the idea called for a first wave of 6,000 troops to land in Galway. This first assault would be backed up by a second and then a third wave, again in Galway. Lastly there was to be a final landing of 20,000 soldiers who would come ashore in Connacht. Interestingly, this final invading force was to be made up of a mix of regular troops, conscripts, volunteers – and convicts. The idea of using convicts as troops of the line was, it seems, already in the minds of the French planners, Carnot and Hoche included.[7]

Carnot, in particular, was putting his faith in two things. One, the power and the magical appeal of Hoche's name which was at this time quite as significant as Napoleon Bonaparte's was later to become. Just the mention of his name, Carnot felt, would fuel terror in the eyes of the enemy and confidence in the minds of the French levies. Carnot's second factor was the belief that Ireland was a festering mass of latent revolution. The whole of the country, he believed, would transform itself into a cauldron of fighting fury the moment the people heard of the French landings.

Wolfe Tone was just as adamant – as were Fitzgerald and O'Connor. The United Irishmen, indeed the whole of their benighted, oppressed and tragic island, they insisted, would rise to help the French bring liberty and freedom to the land. It was what Tone and the others dearly wanted to believe and so it became not the stuff of their fevered dreams, but of reality.

More objective analysis might have indicated that Tone, Fitzgerald and O'Connor were working in the realms of fantasy rather than the hard facts that were needed. Unfortunately, Hoche and Carnot were also caught up in the burning desire to defeat the British and seemed unable to look at the plan without the gleam of fanaticism creeping into their eyes.

The original idea was to combine the Irish invasion with support for Tippoo Sahib, the Indian Prince who was fighting against the British in India. An expedition would be despatched to the sub-continent where it would join up with Tippoo and cause major problems for the government. It was also to be accompanied by another invasion, this time involving 60,000 troops of the line, somewhere in mainland Britain. The whole concept was sheer madness and the logistics would have been impossible.

Fortunately, Hoche was able to use his influence to cancel both the projected aid for Tippoo Sahib and the landing in Britain and concentrate just on Ireland. There had to be a payback, however, and the number of troops to be made available to Hoche was now significantly reduced.

Numbers – of troops, ships and supplies – were crucially important. Quite apart from the pleading of the United Irishmen, one of the main reasons for mounting the attack at this time was the sudden superiority, in numbers, of the French fleet.

Since the beginning of the Revolutionary Wars Britain had always possessed more ships of the line than the French, 113 compared to just 76. The Royal Navy did not just have superiority in numbers. In style and design, in their weapons and tactics, the British ships and sailors were markedly better than their French counterparts.[8] To the strategists of the time these facts were a given and it was something with which they had always had to work.

The plans of Carnot and Hoche had already been set back by several months following the British naval victory at the Battle of the Glorious First of June (1794) when superior seamanship and the heavier weight of the British broadside had wreaked havoc with the French ships. The British victory reinforced the notion that superior ships and larger numbers were important considerations, facts always to be borne in mind. However, things were about to change.

In May 1795 the Dutch fleet was annexed to the French navy and within twelve months Republican maritime might was further enlarged by the addition of the Spanish fleet. For the first time in living memory the French had achieved numerical superiority over the British.

The Dutch and Spanish fleets may not have brought better ship design or seamanship but in an age when naval battle tactics consisted, in the main, of drawing in as close as possible to the enemy and blowing him to bits before he did the same to you, the addition of several dozen extra warships was a major advantage to any navy. The French seized them with alacrity.

Command of the seas around her coast had always given the British an almost mythical sense of immunity but now, at last, that impregnable and previously unbreakable power seemed to be at risk. With more men-of-war than their deadliest enemy there really seemed to be a possibility of French victory – as long as her generals and admirals acted with speed, courage and daring.

Hoche and Carnot were well aware of the sudden improvement in their situation. At the back of their minds there was always the knowledge that the French armies had repeatedly thrown back the cream of European soldiery – why should the British be any different?

And so preparations for the attack on Ireland reached their final stage. The initial idea of a series of landings in Ireland was now significantly altered and modified, in line with the reduced number of soldiers that were to be made available to Hoche.

There would be just one assault, somewhere in the Bantry Bay area. The invading army, all good quality soldiers and well experienced men drawn from the three armies Hoche had under his command, would be carried in a fleet of seventeen vessels. A number of escorting ships, sloops and corvettes, would accompany the invasion fleet. The soldiers would bring with them weapons, ammunition and supplies for the United Irishmen that, Tone continued to insist, would be there to meet the invaders.

Fear of the Royal Navy had never quite gone away, however. Their ships might be outnumbered but all French sailors remained in awe of the British wooden walls and guns. They were also wary of the prowess of their British counterparts, both as seamen and as fighters.

Consequently it was decided that there should be two diversionary raids, assaults that would pull the British ships away from the scene of the important landing in Ireland.

Those raids were a crucial element of the Directory's new plan but even at this early stage it was clear that the two diversionary attacks were to be made by men who were expendable. They were, in fact, little more than a forlorn hope and with that in mind these two forces would be made up largely of convicts and criminals just released from the prisons of northern France.

Chapter 4

Diversion and Attack

Short, sharp guerrilla-style raids on the coast of mainland Europe were not uncommon during the nineteenth century. Russian galleys had carried out numerous raids, both heavy and light, on the coast of Sweden from the early 1700s onwards, despite the presence of large fleets and many ships of the line. The very nature of the raids – hit and run enterprises that were designed to confuse as well as hurt the enemy – meant that the attackers were often back home before the Swedes realised what was taking place.

During the present conflict, even the British, using Marines and sailors, raided the French coast on a number of occasions. Such interventions were troublesome and costly to defend against. Never being intended for long-term occupations the raids were still psychologically damaging for the French, but hugely rewarding for the British and for the émigré soldiers who sometimes accompanied them.

The lessons had been learned and a Swedish officer by the name of Muskeyn, now serving with the French army, came up with a suggestion that was received with interest by the Directory:

> He had seen service with the Russian galleys in the Baltic – vessels that had played a considerable role in that sea from the time of Peter the Great onwards – and suggested the building of craft, on the general line of the 'light Liburnian' galleys of the Greeks, for the transportation of troops.[1]

The Directory noted the suggestion. If an invasion was to take place, such boats would be useful. But it was not quite as simple as building a fleet of lighters or barges and sending them to invade Britain.

Assaults on the coast of Sweden and other European powers – yes, the Directory could see the sense and value of that. Attacks on the island fortress of Britain – well, that was a rather different matter. From galleys in the Baltic to cross-Channel shipping that was able to stand the vagaries of the area, could they really be considered in the same breath?

More than that, the British had always believed their island to be virtually impregnable. Foreign powers attacked it with the full knowledge that such temerity would elicit not just a major effort from the defenders but, at some stage in the future, sure and certain revenge.

Hoche and Carnot were well aware of the risks they were taking but they considered the odds and, perhaps reluctantly, perhaps not totally convinced themselves, decided that the end game – the invasion of Ireland – was worth the risk. And so the planning went ahead. Orders were given for the construction of craft like the ones Muskeyn had suggested at Dunkirk, Calais, Cherbourg and Boulogne.

The first diversionary raid was to involve an attack on Newcastle, then a vitally important centre of industry. Led by General Quantin, the Legion Franche had been originally intended for Cornwall but this, like so much else in what was already proving a very 'leaky' operation was abandoned as being too risky. Newcastle was selected instead where Quantin was ordered to burn the docks, destroy whatever shipping he could find and, in particular, cause irreparable damage to the coal mining industry of the region.

The second raid was to be directed against Bristol; the town was to be sacked and the Legion Noire was then to march on Liverpool and carry out the same exercise there. If a landing at Bristol was impossible the French commander should, according to his orders, come ashore in Wales which, according to intelligence, was a hot bed of dissatisfaction.

For the two diversionary raids to have any real effect there had to be good liaison between Hoche and the two commanders. It was all about timing and anyone looking at the operation with a degree of objectivity could see that this was clearly lacking.

Hoche and his invasion force left Brest on 16 December 1796. The invasion force consisted of 15,000 men, less than originally intended but still a formidable and frightening prospect for those in charge of the defence of Ireland. As well as infantry there was artillery and a plentiful supply of ammunition but from the beginning things began to go badly wrong.

The French fleet, despite being made up of seventeen ships of the line and nineteen support vessels, was not as powerful as might, at first, be supposed.

Admiral Villeneuve, later Lord Nelson's opponent at Trafalgar, was delayed in making the passage from Toulon which meant that men and equipment intended for the expedition never made it to Brest. Villeneuve and the men of the recently co-opted Spanish fleet were unhappy and unwilling to leave the relative safety of the Mediterranean and the sea lanes they knew. Again, they delayed and prevaricated, anything rather than set to sea. Those sailors who were waiting on the ships at Brest had to be partitioned out in order to fill empty spaces and as a result many of the huge three-decked warships sailed without full crews.

Morard de Galles, the Admiral in charge of Hoche's ships, had spent a long time in prison during the period of the Terror and although he was an efficient and capable officer he was also beset by bad health and a degree of timidity. Such personal weaknesses had no place in an operation like this. Above all, Morard de Galles was terrified of meeting a British squadron at sea and in an attempt to avoid any enemy frigates that might be lurking off Brest he decided to leave harbour by the little used Passage du Raz.

Confusion over which course to take saw some ships head to the south first before swinging around and driving for the western approaches. Other vessels took a more direct course. It meant that the fleet was scattered from the start.

Then the weather played a hand – as it so often did in any attempted invasion of Britain. Queen Elizabeth knew how influential the weather had been in the defeat of the Spanish Armada in 1688, causing a medal to be struck bearing the legend 'God blew and they were scattered'. The same sentiment could have been uttered in 1796.

As soon as the French were at sea strong winds and violent storms smashed into the ships. These were some of the worst storms seen for years and they caused havoc. Hoche and Morard de Galles on board the frigate *Fraternite* were swept out into the Atlantic, in the process losing touch with all of the ships in the squadron. The French fleet was badly battered, many of them losing sails and other equipment in the storm, and the entire force was soon spread out across the ocean like toy ships on the nursery room floor.

By good fortune and good seamanship most of the fleet did somehow manage to rendezvous in Bantry Bay on 20 and 21 December – with the notable exception of Hoche and Morard de Galles who were still being driven westwards out in the Atlantic. Command of the fleet now lay in the hands of Rear Admiral Bouvet but he, like his superior officer, was also labouring under a cloak of timidity. Hoche's deputy and second in command of the entire expedition was Emanuel Grouchy. The fate of the enterprise now came down to him and to Admiral Bouvet.

Wolfe Tone, on board the *Indomitable*, was ecstatic. As he stared out at the coast of his native land once more he could be excused for glowing with pleasure. All of his plans had been leading to this – wide empty invasion beaches, the sea gentle and the wind light. On board the ships were 15,000 troops of the line, the finest fighting men in France, and if Hoche might be missing, the lack of opposition on those golden beaches more than made up for the loss.

Tone had got it wrong, there was actually some opposition but it was severely limited. Ensign Richard White, a local land owner, and thirty Yeomanry troops provided the only British forces in the area. There were no regular soldiers within 200 miles of Bantry Bay and Admiral Kingsmill at Cork – 100 miles to the north – had only one ship of the line and a few frigates with which to oppose the invaders.[2]

Ensign White had gathered together his part-time troops the minute French sails were spotted off the coast. Wolfe Tone now confidently expected his United Irishmen also to follow suit and come racing to the area. It did not happen.

The non-appearance of his supporters was, Tone felt, worrying but not disastrous. The United Irishmen were clearly waiting to see what the French would do before committing themselves to what was, at the end of the day, an act of treason. A swift landing, the destruction of

White's puny army and the establishment of a strong bridgehead on the Irish coast would, Tone believed, bring them running. None of it happened.

Emanuel Grouchy decided that he would wait for the reappearance of General Hoche before landing any troops. No amount of argument could persuade him to show initiative and disembark. He would stick to his guns. Meanwhile Ensign White marched his men up and down the sand, hurling abuse at the anchored French ships but there was no response.

Unfortunately for Grouchy and for Hoche, out in the Atlantic the storm had worsened. The *Fraternite* was so badly battered that she almost sank and every minute saw Hoche blown further and further away from his command.

Off the beaches of Bantry Bay the situation was also now becoming desperate. The calm seas that had so pleased Wolfe Tone had gradually become choppy as the wind rose. It was obvious to everyone that the longer the ships rode at anchor the less chance there seemed of the troops ever getting ashore. For two weeks the French battleships and transports lurched and strained at their anchor cables as White marched, Tone fretted and Grouchy remained unperturbed.

Just as with Knox receiving news of the later French landings at Fishguard, so this episode in the story is another reminder of the Battle of Waterloo. In 1815 Grouchy once again had the fate of all Europe in his hands and yet again he failed to take his chance. Pursuing the retreating Prussians on Napoleon's right flank Grouchy heard the sound of guns and knew that his Emperor was in combat.

Despite Napoleon's instructions to march to the sound of the guns, Grouchy continued with his pursuit of Blucher's army. Consequently, Napoleon was kept at bay all day and when Blucher's Prussians finally arrived on the field ahead of Grouchy the French defeat was assured.

It could be argued that Grouchy was just an unlucky general. Napoleon himself, upon being recommended to appoint one particular Marshal (not Grouchy) to a new command, listened to all of the man's attributes and skills and then asked, 'Yes, but is he lucky?' The Emperor certainly knew the value of luck in any military campaign.

Grouchy was not unlucky but he lacked the initiative to change his plans when the situation demanded it and failed to use whatever basic military instinct he possessed. It was a fatal flaw in his character that proved disastrous in 1815 but was equally as damaging off Bantry Bay in 1796.

It is the 'what if' scenario again, but if Grouchy had disembarked, all of Ireland would have been open before him. Then the United Irishmen would undoubtedly have risen and the final result could have been the cessation of the whole country.

The French knew the enormity of the mistake, even if Grouchy did not:

> From 20th December till 6th January French ships had lain at anchor in Bantry Bay … without any opposition from the English cruisers. No important concentration of troops had been made to oppose the army, while the French could have landed 6,400 men on 24th December, 4,000 more on 27th, and another 4,000 between 3rd and 6th January. That is to say that practically all the force could and should have been landed.[3]

Grouchy did nothing. He sat and waited for Hoche. His reasoning was simple – the general had the plans of attack and the various proclamations which it was hoped would bring the Irish to their side. Most important of all, Hoche had the money chest. It should have made no difference but without Hoche there was little heart for the enterprise and so Grouchy hung on, waiting and hoping for a miracle or some form of divine intervention.

The general did finally make it to Bantry Bay, arriving on 30 December. Even before his return it had become clear that the end was nigh. The storm was approaching near-cyclonic proportions and Bouvet and Grouchy decided that enough was enough: 'The order was given for the flagship *Indomitable* to cut her cables and run. One by one the remaining ships followed suit and cleared for France.'[4]

When Hoche finally appeared off the Irish coast the anchorage was already half empty and he had little option but to follow his ships away from what was, in reality, a glorious chance for victory. The invasion of Ireland was over before it even began.

In mainland Britain news of the French attempt was beginning to spread. Early in the New Year, Lord Cawdor, on his estate at Stackpole in Pembrokeshire, noted somewhat laconically in his diary 'French fleet in Bantry Bay'.[5] The response was not always so laid back.

Lord Bridport received news of the French presence while he was sitting on board his flagship with the fleet at Spithead. He immediately weighed anchor and arrived in Bantry Bay two days after the last French vessel had left the area. It was a warning for the British – the Royal Navy needed to be better positioned or disposed.

The only British naval commander to achieve contact with the fleeing enemy was Sir Edward Pellew, the famous frigate captain. Sweeping the sea lanes he came across the French seventy-four *Droits de l'Homme* and drove her ashore on the coast of Brittany. A large number of French sailors and soldiers were drowned as the ship was smashed to pieces in the breakers.

Several other vessels, transports and frigates, were wrecked on the Irish coast as they tried to beat before the wind and make it back to France. Altogether, over 4,000 Frenchmen either lost their lives or were taken prisoner.[6]

Wolfe Tone was one of the lucky ones. He made it back to France but was furious at what he rightly considered a lost opportunity. He had been almost swept overboard and drowned when a huge wave lashed the *Indomitable*. It was the closest he had come to losing his life and he was to write bitterly that he had not seen a single British warship during the whole sorry episode. The only troops he had seen were Ensign White and his part-time Yeomen – and that was from a distance.

The failure did not destroy Tone's ambitions, however. He was soon involved in other schemes to free Ireland but none of them had the same opportunities for victory as the expedition of 1796.

His end was inevitable. In 1798, during another attempt to invade Ireland, his ship *Hoche* was intercepted at sea by Sir John Warren and after a ten-hour battle Tone was taken prisoner. Court martialled, he was condemned to death for treason but despite his commission in the French army it was decided that he should be hanged as a traitor, not shot.

With courage and the indomitable spirit that were typical of the man, Tone refused to give the British the pleasure of seeing him 'dance on the end of a rope'. He cheated the hangman by cutting his throat with a pen knife. It took him two days to die.

Hoche's attempted invasion of Ireland had met with total disaster. For the two diversionary raids, originally intended to take place at the same time as Hoche's ill-fated attempt on what was grandly referred to as 'Great Britain's other island', there was mixed fortune.

Firstly there was the Legion Franche. The flat bottomed barges that were intended to carry General Quantin and his troops were built and in position at Dunkirk by the beginning of October 1796. The plan was for them to sail silently into Dutch waters before striking across the North Sea towards Great Yarmouth. From there they would hug the coast to avoid the Royal Navy patrols and head to Newcastle and the River Tyne.

A force of 5,000 troops was assembled in north eastern France but many of these were low-grade conscripts and convicts who had little or no interest in the proposed attack: 'In October the general reported that 1,500 men had deserted and "those who remain say openly they would rather be chopped into pieces than set foot on board those flat boats".'[7]

Most of the deserters were quickly rounded up and herded back onto their barges where they waited, sullen, still mutinous and muttering about their likely fate.

Finally, towards the end of November a start was made. The strange-looking fleet, wallowing uncomfortably in the swell and with most of the soldiers already seasick, headed out past the mole at Dunkirk. The people of the town watched them go, shaking their heads in disbelief and happy to see these seemingly uncontrollable ruffians finally leave their quiet community.

Slowly the barges struggled along the coast to Flushing. The mood of the soldiers who were battened down and incarcerated in the holds of the barges had got no better. The journey was not long but it was unpleasant enough to convince the members of the Legion Franche that soldiering was a lot better than serving as sailors. At Flushing the barges were met by a flotilla of frigates ready to escort them across the North Sea.

At this stage the weather once again took a hand. The wind and sea got up and the barges quickly became unmanageable. Broken legs and split heads were the order of the day as the troops were thrown around like corks. The soldiers of the Legion Franche were, by now, terrified and on the verge of mutiny. As one man they rounded on the sailors who handled the transports and forced them to turn back to land.

General Quantin's own vessel was wrecked in the chaos and although he managed to swim ashore, half drowned and furious, it was clear that the raid on Newcastle was going nowhere. Even to the rather blinkered eyes of the Directory it was apparent that no further use could be made, either of the invasion barges or of the Legion Franche. The Legion was disbanded, the barges laid up or sunk and the expedition abandoned.

The attempt by the Legion Franche to cause chaos in the north of England had foundered. Just like Hoche's expedition to Bantry Bay it had ended before it had really begun. That left only the Legion Noire, still forming and gathering in the fields and fortresses of Brest.

Chapter 5

The Legion Noire

Perhaps the strangest part of the whole sorry story of the last invasion of Britain was now about to take place. With the main assault on Ireland and the first diversionary raid to Newcastle both ending in chaos and confusion it would have been logical for the Directory to cancel the remaining expedition to Britain.

To any sane and objective observer, cancellation of the enterprise and disbanding of the unit was the only thing to do. There could be no real purpose in launching an attack. And yet, strangely, that was precisely what Carnot and Hoche now decided to do.

Exactly what benefit they hoped to gain remains unclear. Possibly, having begun gathering together convicts and other desperate ruffians, the Directory realised that they had collected and positioned all of their 'bad eggs' in one basket. Several hundred difficult and amoral criminals in one place presented a formidable problem and what to do with the fruits of its creation could well have given nightmares to the members of the Directory. There remains no proof that this was one answer to the quandary but it does seem possible.

The expedition would certainly be a forlorn hope, that much was obvious, a last desperate throw of the dice involving men who were dispensable but who were desperate enough to make some sort of mark in Britain. Wolfe Tone wrote in his diary about the mischief the raiding force might achieve in Britain but admitted, to himself at least, that ultimately the men of the Legion Noire would be rounded up and caught.

Recent writers have questioned the idea that the Legion was made up largely of convicts, claiming that many of the troops were quality soldiers. The reply to that is yes – and no. The concept of taking disaffected criminals and sending them on guerrilla attacks was something that the French Republic had already thought about, several times. There was a degree of method in their madness.

Earlier in the year a small raiding party of convicts under the command of Pierre Joseph Macheret was put together to attack either Cornwall or west Wales and cause as much damage as possible before being wiped out. Their reward, if any of the convict soldiers survived, was to be sent to start a new life on one of the French possessions in the West Indies. Macheret was a complete villain, one of the worst rogues in the country, a man 'of whom France might well be purged'. His convict soldiers were no better.[1]

The Macheret scheme eventually came to nothing but now, with the Irish expedition a failure and the raid on Newcastle in ruins, Hoche began to seriously consider the benefits of once more using criminals and deserters in a task of war.

He wrote to the Directory outlining his intentions and describing what he called a second legion of irregulars:

> It is composed of six hundred men from all the prisons in my district, and they are collected in two forts or islands to obviate the possibility of their escape. I associate with them picked convicts from the galleys, still wearing their irons.[2]

The leader of this inglorious band of warriors was to be an Irish-American soldier by the name of William Tate. Little is known about the man who was to lead this last invasion. Even his age is uncertain, some accounts placing him at close to 70, others nearer 40. At that time and in that place, even somebody just over the age of 40 would have been regarded as old so it is, perhaps, easy to see why a mistake could be made.

One thing is known for sure. Tate had fought for the American revolutionaries during the War of Independence and hated the British with a vengeance.

His forefathers came from the Wexford area of Ireland but Tate had spent most of his life in the Colonies where his dislike of the British was apparently fostered by the murder of his family at the hands of Native Americans in the pay of the British government. That at least was the story he put around; how much truth there was in the tale is questionable.

William Tate first appears in the pages of history when he was commissioned into the 4th South Carolina Regiment as a Lieutenant in May 1778. This was an artillery regiment, the only artillery unit in the whole of the Carolinas available to Washington's Continental Army. Eighteen months after gaining his commission Tate was promoted to the rank of Captain.

In some quarters Tate's conduct during his military service was apparently exemplary. However, there is also evidence to the contrary. In March 1780 it seems that he was arrested for making an improper return. Mistake or attempt at fraud, he was reprimanded but nothing further is known about the incident.[3]

Tate spent his war in the south and it is possible that he was present at the Battle of Savannah when over a thousand rebels were killed during an assault on the city. It was the British Army's biggest and most significant victory of the war. Tate was then captured in an attack on nearby Charleston and later released as part of an exchange of prisoners. After that he seemingly served without incident until the end of the war.

Following the cessation of hostilities William Tate was awarded a pension of $1,100 and given a grant of 300 acres of land. He bought more land with his newly acquired wealth and settled down to life as a farmer on the banks of the Kiowa River close to Orchard in the state of Colorado. The peaceful life was not something he enjoyed, however, and it was not long before a restless William Tate was on the move once more.

In 1793 he became involved in a French scheme to free Louisiana and Florida from Spanish control. Tate's part in the plan had been to launch and oversee an attack on St Augustine on the eastern coast of Florida while further attacks, planned to divert and disrupt Spanish attention, were made on other ill-defined points on the Gulf coast. There were certainly shades here of Hoche's later plan for a series of raids on Britain and Ireland – it seems that Tate did not learn from his mistakes.

The armies never marched and the affair came to an unfortunate end. Tate lost a considerable amount of money that he had spent on weapons, supplies and salaries.

He had also been authorised to raise and train a force of frontiersmen for an attack on New Orleans. The cost of this was supposed to be borne by France but when the two schemes fell apart Tate had not been paid a penny. To make matters worse he now proceeded to make several bad investments with a land company which promptly crashed and burned.

He was not just in a bad economic position, his designs and machinations had put Tate into a very bad light with the new American government. They were embarrassed and annoyed at the ease with which French agents had combined with people like Tate to foment armed conflict within the boundaries of the United States. For a newly created country, still in danger of future war with Britain, this was publicity they certainly did not need.

By the summer of 1795 Tate found himself in a desperate position. He had married eight years before but by the time of the Louisiana affair there was no mention of a wife. His will gave most of his property and possessions to his nephew and the assumption is that by 1795 she had either died or the couple had separated.

In June 1795 Tate decided that he would leave America and seek refuge in France. Not only was such a move politically expedient – the US government was becoming more aggressive by the day – there was also the matter of trying to recover at least some of the money he had laid out in recruiting soldiers for the French Republic. At least in France he would be closer to the source of revenue and he could use his undoubted charm to put pressure on government officials.

* * *

Tate arrived in Paris in the summer of 1795 and quickly made himself known to the Irish rebels in the city. Wolfe Tone apparently moved into a house just a few doors away from Tate and together they began badgering French officials with schemes and ideas to cause problems for Britain.[4] One idea was to launch French troops in an attack against Bermuda and Jamaica but this, like so many of Tate's other schemes, one of which was to transport soldiers across the Channel inside gigantic hollow wheels, came to nothing.

Historians and writers like J.E. Thomas have made great play of the fact that Tate spoke no French, using the limitation as one of many reasons why his choice as chef de brigade was so strange.[5] A total deficiency in the language is unlikely. Tate may not have been fluent but having spent several months in Paris and with a history of working and scheming in the French-speaking parts of America he would almost certainly have had some knowledge of the language.

By now Tate was also pestering the French government to confirm his commission in their army. He had been given this at the time of the planned Louisiana affair but so far it had proved to be nothing more than a paper exercise. Confirmation of his commission would mean money and status and William Tate was now in need of both. For some time he had been petitioning the government to recover the money he had spent on their behalf but, again, nothing had been forthcoming.

Pamela Horn has stated that when William Tate was made chef du brigade of the Legion Noire it may well have been that Hoche came up with his name, not because of his military prowess but because he had been making such a damned nuisance of himself: 'It may be that the French government was not unhappy to see its uninvited guest leave their shores.'[6]

That, clearly, is surmise but it would make sense. If the Legion Noire was a disposable asset, why should their leader be any different? That was not what Hoche said in public, however. In a letter to the Directory he referred to Tate as 'a man of ability, an ex-soldier.'[7]

Having finally received his commission William Tate could sit back and look at the soldiers under his command. Whichever way he looked at it, his troops were something of a rabble army.

To begin with, their uniforms were makeshift and patchy. In the main the soldiers were clad in the uniform jackets that had been captured when the British expedition to Quiberon had failed in 1795.

They had been dyed black but it was poorly done and the original red colour showed through on many of them. Witnesses later called the jackets 'rust coloured'. Overall though there was enough black or dark-brown clothing to give the unit its commonly used name, the Legion Noire.

Their correct nomenclature was the Deuxieme Legion de Francs although Hoche, in his orders to Tate, gave them the name La Seconde Legion de Francs. Estimates of their exact number also vary. In his Instructions to Colonel Tate, Hoche states: 'There will be placed under the command of Colonel Tate, a body of troops, completely organised, numbering one thousand and fifty, all resolute and determined men.'[8]

In the wake of the invasion a return of prisoner numbers made by Lieutenant General James Rooke gave the figures of forty-six officers and 1,178 men. In addition Tate admitted to twelve casualties.[9] If those figures are correct – and this would probably have been the most accurate assessment – it would give the battalion strength of the Legion Noire as 1236 officers and men.

In his calculations, from observation rather than accurate counting, Wolfe Tone put the figure at 1,800, calling them all brigands and desperadoes. Other estimates say that Tate had at his disposal 600 regulars and 800 irregular troops. The regulars were what have been called 'half decent Revolutionary volunteers'. Of these, approximately 200 were grenadiers, men whom Lord Cawdor was later to describe as all being over 6ft in height and 'as fine a body of men as I have set eyes on'.[10]

Tate's grenadiers were certainly an impressive group of men. Traditionally the tallest and most able of the soldiers in any French army, grenadiers were the backbone of all French military units – and were to remain so until the time of Napoleon's later defeat at Waterloo.

The grenadiers of the Legion Noire were organised into two elite units and were identifiable by their red epaulettes and plumed helmets. They were tough and experienced soldiers who must have looked at their convict colleagues with wonder and disgust.

The Legion was divided into two battalions, each comprising five Chasseur Companies and one of grenadiers. The chasseurs (the name meaning the hunters) were light infantry and this was where most of the irregular troops – or convicts – had been placed.

There was a sort of perverted logic in using this troublesome element of society as an avenging or invading force. It was a policy that had been in force since the days of the 'armee revolutionairre' when the Jacobins exported their most troublesome citizens out of Paris into the countryside. It limited the possibility of further armed revolt and counter revolution in the capital and at the same time it decreased the surplus population. In that way the constant problem of supplying sufficient provisions for the people of Paris was reduced.

To inflict such ruffians on the British people seemed, at least to those who had witnessed the effect of British interference in the Vendee, to be poetic justice of the finest sort.

It was not just the convicts who caused Tate concerns. An order had gone out from Hoche to all of the army commanders in his region – he wanted more soldiers to 'pad out' the Legion and expressly asked his commanders to send more troops to Brest. The commanders did as they were bid but, like all army officers, took liberties with the general's orders. There was no way they were ever going to send him their best troops and what Tate and Hoche now got was a combination of troublemakers, shirkers and ne'er-do-wells.

What it all meant was that apart from his grenadiers and a handful of regulars who were at least willing to try their best, around half of the Legion Noire was unprepared and unwilling to take part in any sort of action against the British. A more unlikely gathering of troops had probably never before embarked on an act of war.

Tate's officers were a little better but they were still, in the main, either inexperienced or half-hearted in their intentions. A French document held in the Carmarthen Records Office, as well as stating that there were 1,233 troops in the Legion, lists the officer corps as twelve captains, twelve lieutenants and twelve sous or sub lieutenants. Tate had the services of two aides de camp.[11]

His second in command, the Chef de Bataillon of one of the two Brigades, was a man by the name of Jacques-Phillippe Le Brun. An aristocrat – formerly Le Baron de Rochemure – he had actually served in the Royalist army of Louis XVI and even fought against the Republican forces at Quiberon. By renouncing his hereditary title, Le Brun had avoided the guillotine but had decided on a life as an émigré. In what was an astonishing about face, by 1797 he had transferred his allegiance and now found himself as one of the more experienced members of the Legion Noire.

The journey from defeat at Quiberon to second in command of the Legion Noire must have been difficult and tortuous but somehow Le Brun managed it. Presumably taken prisoner after the disaster, he must have used all of his skills as a diplomat and man of the world to escape jail and begin a new phase of his life.

Le Brun's heart was not with the Republican cause, however, and why he had chosen to join up with Tate's band of scallywags in the Legion has never been made clear. If nothing else it was probably the most effective way of escaping from France. Half-hearted and indolent, Le Brun was one of the main advocates of surrender and his sole contribution to the expedition seems to have been carrying the request for terms to Lord Cawdor.

Many of the other officers were émigrés who had been captured and were now released from captivity on the condition that they took part in the expedition. They were, presumably, taking the main chance, joining the expedition in the hope of quietly slipping away at the first opportunity.

Also included in the list of officers were three rebel Irishmen. They were not members of Tone's United Irishmen but they had no love for Britain. As such, they were possibly some of the more reliable members of the Legion Noire.

Robert Morrison was a 35-year-old captain from Bangor in County Down. Since the age of 16 he had been employed as a servant to various French aristocrats but when war broke out he was working as a turner in Calais. Before long he found himself conscripted into the French army and, as a natural speaker of English and French, soon gravitated to Tates's Legion Noire.

The second Irish officer of note was Nicholas Tyrell. Also a captain – and also aged 35 – Tyrell came from St Margaret's in the

Dublin area but when war erupted he was living with his aunt in France. He was working as a currier but, like Morrison, he soon found himself conscripted and, in due course, sent to the Legion Noire.

Both Morrison and Tyrell later gave evidence before the magistrate Richard Ford at Whitehall, both of them claiming that when they enlisted in the Legion Noire, neither of them were aware that their destination was Wales. Both men had been intended to sail with Hoche to Ireland but, despite taking ship on the *Cassard*, they were ordered ashore again. They were needed, it seemed, to act as interpreters on Tate's forthcoming enterprise.

Interestingly, a man by the name of Nathaniel Oliver, a warder or turnkey at the House of Correction in Cold Bath Fields, London, also gave evidence to Ford, stating that he knew Tyrell:

> He verily believes the above named, N. Tyrell, has been seen by the examinant at the 'Magpie and Stump', a recruiting house in Clerkenwell, about two years since, when he appeared to be acting as a recruiting Sergeant. [He] says that many persons in the said House of Correction have informed the examinant that they have seen Tyrell before.[12]

Nathaniel Oliver may well have been correct. He could have been looking for no particular gain by lying but nothing seems to have been done about his deposition. It might shed some light, however, on the character of this and other Irish members of the Legion.

The third Irish officer was the 20-year-old Lieutenant Barry St Leger. A native of Limerick he had been sent to America when he was only 12, working and living with his uncle, Bryan Smith, on his farm some forty or fifty miles from Charleston in South Carolina. In November 1795 he returned to Britain with a cargo of rice that he intended to sell on the London market and pass on the proceeds to his mother who was still living just outside Limerick.

Unfortunately his ship lost her rudder in a storm and he was wrecked off the western coast of Ireland. His cargo was swept away by the swirling breakers. After staying with his mother for a month,

St Leger decided to return to America but his ship, the *Sally* of Boston was taken by a French privateer called *La Vengeur*. He was imprisoned at Brest and was languishing there when by sheer chance he met Colonel Tate.

St Leger and Tate had known each other in America and the colonel was easily able to arrange St Leger's release from prison. He promptly joined the Irish Brigade, was present during the abortive raid on Bantry Bay and was about to join the army of the Sambre and Meuse when Tate granted him a commission in the Legion Noire.[13]

Like Morrison and Tyrell, after the surrender and their imprisonment St Leger also gave a deposition to Robert Ford, a detailed statement that offers a fascinating account of the Legion's activities in and around Fishguard. St Leger was young and totally inexperienced but he does seem, from his own deposition and from other sources, to be the one man who at least attempted to act like a soldier during the three days of the invasion. It is hard not to place him as the hero of the hour – in an episode in history where heroes were sadly lacking that is some accolade.

There may well have been other Irishmen serving in the Legion but as other ranks were neither listed nor named it is impossible to make accurate judgements about this.

Tate's orders were clear. They had supposedly been translated and copied out by no less a hand than Wolfe Tone's. He certainly claimed to have made the copy, long and detailed as it was, but such a claim does depend on Tone's ability as a French speaker. Transcribing written orders was not something you wanted to get wrong.

General Hoche had been clear what he wanted from the Legion Noire even if the original orders were written some time before the operation began. They could certainly have benefited from either a rewrite or, at most, some slight modification. As it happened they got neither:

> The expedition under the command of Colonel Tate has in
> view three principal objects: the first is, if possible, to raise
> an insurrection in the country; the second is to interrupt

and embarrass the commerce of the enemy; and the third is
to prepare and facilitate the way for a descent by distracting
the attention of the English government.[14]

Reading that last point it still seems as if Hoche had clearly not given
up on the idea of diverting the Royal Navy, nor of undertaking another
landing himself. Or had he? It is more than likely that the order had
been left in, unchanged since the early days of the plan.

Coming ashore in the rural areas that lined the southern shores
of the Bristol Channel, Tate was to land in the daytime, wait for night
before forming up his troops, and then march on Bristol:

Colonel Tate is to advance rapidly in the dark, on the side of
Bristol which may be to windward, and immediately set fire
to that quarter. If the enterprise be conducted with dexterity,
it cannot fail to produce the total ruin of the town, the port,
the docks and the vessels, and to strike terror and amazement
into the very heart of the capital of England.[15]

Once this was achieved, Tate was to leave Bristol burning and devastated
behind him. He was ordered to re-embark his troops on the fleet –
which was to wait for his return – and cross over the Bristol Channel
to the Welsh side of the estuary.

Having achieved this objective and keeping Cardiff always on his
right, he was to march north through the Welsh hinterland towards
Chester and Liverpool, maintaining the discipline of his troops but
burning and pillaging as he went.

He was, the orders read, to break down bridges, burn any
shipping or convoys of food he might encounter and destroy roads
and causeways that could be used to transport troops. Enemy
arsenals where guns and ammunition were stored should be burned
or otherwise destroyed. If, on his march, he should encounter militia
he was to wipe them out.

The aim, then, was clear. Tate was to raise the countryside, rally
the populace to his flag and fan the spark which would bring down

William Pitt and the whole British government. Hoche was clear about the emotional value of the expedition:

> In all countries the poor are the class most prone to insurrection, and this disposition is to be forwarded by distributing money and drink; by inveighing against the government as the cause of public distress; by recommending and facilitating a rising to plunder the public stores and magazines, and the property of the rich, whose affluence is the natural subject envy of the poor.[16]

To assist in the first of these objectives, the Legion Noire was well supplied with barrels of brandy but it had little to speak of in the way of rations. The French army had always, traditionally, foraged for its food. It was a short-sighted approach that was to haunt the armies of France for many years. As far as Tate was concerned it was to be an important factor in the days ahead.

Significantly, the way the orders were written, the 'coup de main' on Bristol was only to be attempted if the wind and tide allowed it and if the Channel was undefended. Otherwise the fleet would bypass the Severn and sail up St George's Channel between Ireland and Wales.

If that should be the case Tate would come ashore somewhere on Cardigan Bay, in an area that was not well defended and, on paper at least, seems to have had few strategic advantages. No specific location was mentioned just the 'catch all' of Cardigan Bay.

It is unlikely that Hoche or Carnot had any specific understanding or knowledge of what the land and the people on the bay were like. Even from the briefest of studies, maps of the area showed it to be a godforsaken region. But from there Tate's march on Chester and Liverpool would be, arguably, even easier than if he set out from the south coast of Wales.

There was also a suggestion that Tate should consider marching north to link up with General Quantin in Northumberland. If such a move was to be made, said Hoche, he must be informed by a message being sent to him in Ireland where he would be making war on Britain with the aid of the United Irishmen. Clearly, nobody had thought of redrafting the orders in light of the failed Irish expedition and Quantin's debacle at Flushing.

Tate was nobody's fool and when he read the orders he must have realised that the Directory – and Hoche in particular – had lost interest in his Legion Noire. He must have realised that he had become yesterday's man.

In the fluctuating and tentative political world of Republican France people and ideas had short lives – today's hero could very easily become tomorrow's villain unless somebody was willing to take up their cause and keep it at the forefront of the Directory's agile brain. There had been many examples of men who had fallen quickly from grace.

Indeed, Hoche himself had already received his own marching orders from the Directory. His star was on the wane but, even so, he had been appointed to take command of the Army of the Sambre and Meuse and by the time Tate finally sailed, he was long gone from western France.

Nevertheless, Tate had his instructions. They may have been a little contradictory in parts but in other respects they were crystal clear. He was to bring chaos and confusion to the hearts of his bitterest foe.

Gathering together his troops and supplies had proved a difficult time for Colonel William Tate. Just keeping the men in order had been far from easy. The convicts had been given their freedom solely to launch an attack on Britain and many of them must have felt it was a poisoned chalice. While they were detained in prison they were relatively easily controlled but once they transferred to the ships prior to setting out, indiscipline quickly showed.

On the day before they sailed one of the convicts broke out of the ship, sold his uniform in order to get money for drink and attempted to start a mutiny. Le Brun ordered that his punishment was to be made to run the gauntlet between lines of his comrades, all armed with knotted ropes. By having the man beaten senseless Le Brun probably felt that he and all members of the Legion Noire had learned their lesson. He should have known better.

Meanwhile Colonel Tate was sitting in his lodgings, contentedly reading his orders. At this stage he still had hopes of a dramatic success.

Warmed by these orders William Tate finally boarded the *Vengeance*, the ship that would transport him to Britain and to glory. It was 16 February 1797 and it was time to go and make war.

Chapter 6

Towards Fishguard

Having herded the members of the Legion Noire onto the ships, reluctant recruits and willing participants alike, matters immediately stalled, at least for a short while. The wind and tides were against them. Tate was infuriated that it wasn't until two days later that the wind was finally in the right quarter.

The delay was all the more infuriating because everything was ready – troops, weapons and supplies – and only Britain's greatest ally, the weather, was now holding things up. Tate fumed as he strode up and down the poop deck of the *Vengeance*.

'Patience, Colonel,' the naval commander told him. 'The weather will change.'

'Yes,' Tate responded, 'but when?'

Like William Tate, Commodore Jean Joseph Castagnier was a veteran of the American War of Independence. In his case he had served as a privateer captain, preying on British merchantmen for the French and American governments. He was a capable and charming man and a more than competent sailor who had gone on to serve with Hoche during the defence of Dunkirk, the action that had made the general's name. Like Lazarre Hoche, he had achieved rapid promotion and was now in charge of the small fleet or squadron that was to carry the Legion Noire to Britain.

Two of his ships, the *Vengeance* and the *Resistance*, were virtually brand-new frigates. Larger than the British vessels of a similar designation, the two ships had been built in 1794 and 1796 respectively. They were the only vessels in their class, each carrying twenty-eight 18 pounder and twelve 8 pounder cannons. They had crews of 340 men. The *Vengeance* had already seen action but the *Resistance* was making her first trip outside French territorial waters.[1]

In addition to the two powerful frigates, Castagnier's fleet also had the services of the *Constance*, a twenty-four gun corvette, and the *Vautour*, a small 14-gun lugger. It was an efficient and well-equipped naval force, crewed by skilled seamen and commanded by a man who knew his business. He certainly knew the weather around Brest.

Castagnier had been right, the weather did finally change and as dusk fell on 18 February the ships were eventually able to slip their moorings, ease out of their anchorage and head down the Camaret Roads. There was a slight chill in the air, no more than might be expected as the small squadron headed out from land into the Atlantic, but in general the weather was now mild, and the sea calm.

The troops had no idea of their destination – nor did many of the officers. The Irishman Nicholas Tyrell was later to claim that: 'He believed they were destined for the West Indies and says that he knew nothing of being to land in Wales.'[2]

If that was true of Tyrell who, as an Irishman would have had a vested interest in being, at best, economical with the truth, it would certainly be true of the other junior officers as well. They were informed of their destination as the voyage continued – perhaps understandably, nobody even considered telling the rank and file.

Many of the convict soldiers were kept in irons or chains until Camaret Roads and Brest were well behind them. Given the poor discipline of the men it seemed a sensible precaution. At least two accounts of the invasion remarked that the French soldiers who were shortly to be taken prisoner bore the marks of chains on their legs and wrists.[3] In an age of brutal, even barbaric punishment, men would have been used to seeing the marks of fetters and chains on the bodies of criminals so it was not surprising for the people of Pembrokeshire to come across such sights.

After the episode was over Lord Milford, the Lord Lieutenant of the county of Pembrokeshire, wrote to the Duke of Portland regarding the prisoners. He stated that: 'The number of Frenchmen made prisoner exceeded fourteen hundred. Many of these appeared to have the marks of fetters upon their legs.'[4]

Such marks would have lasted for a long time but there was no doubt that Tate and Castagnier were taking no chances with their recalcitrant forces. They had spent months in irons, a few days longer was hardly going to hurt them.

The condition of the convicts that first night at sea – most of them locked securely below decks on one or other of the four ships – must have been unpleasant. Seasickness would have been rife and the only scant consolation the wretched men had was that the mal de mer would have kept away the gnawing pangs of hunger. For Tate, Castagnier and the other officers it also reduced the possibility of any sort of breakout to a non-event.

Progress was steady. By the second afternoon the English coast had been sighted and soon the fleet was off Land's End. In order to hide their true identity Castagnier ordered that his ships should hoist Russian ensigns. Such a ruse was carried out not a moment too soon. As the French fleet rounded the westernmost tip of England and began to cruise along the coast of Cornwall they ran slap into a convoy of British merchant vessels. The two fleets passed close to each other, exchanged brief salutes and went happily on their way.

One small coaster, however, was lagging behind the convoy. Castagnier felt that it had come too close. There was no saying what the British sailors might have seen and, under cover of darkness, he ordered the lugger *Vautour* to double back, overhaul her and send her to the bottom. Better to be safe than sorry, Castagnier told Tate, and by the time she was missed it would be too late, they would have reached their destination.[5]

The *Vautour* wheeled around and soon overhauled the coaster. The English captain and crew were taken on board the French lugger and confined below deck. They were the first prisoners of the campaign. With a few well-aimed cannon shots the British merchant ship was quickly holed and sent to the bottom. First blood in the expedition had gone to the French.

There were several more sightings of merchant shipping as the squadron proceeded slowly up the Bristol Channel. On the morning of 20 February they anchored off Lundy Island to wait for the tide to flood. While anchored there two small coasters out of Ilfracombe came close to the French ships to investigate. They were duly captured and destroyed. Castagnier was later to claim that he had sunk fourteen small merchant vessels during the voyage and in the time spent off Fishguard, their crews being added to the toll of prisoners in the holds of the two frigates.

Unfortunately for the French they were themselves seen and identified several times. Off Lundy the master of the sloop *St Ives* recognised them for what they were and quickly reported the matter to Samuel Hancorne, the Collector for the port of Swansea. Hancorne immediately wrote, reporting the sighting to the Duke of Portland, the Home Secretary. It was all done with alacrity but by the time the message was received the French fleet was already off Fishguard:

> May it please Your Grace to be informed that Mr Andrew Stevens, master of the sloop 'St Ives,' who arrived in harbour this morning has acquainted me that … yesterday about ten in the morning, saw three Ships of War which appeared to be frigates of about 40 guns each, black sided, and a lugger, under an easy sail about two Leagues from the north end of Lundy Island.[6]

Portland received another communication on 23 February, this time from the town of Barnstaple. The town and the people of the coast, it was claimed, had seen the French ships and were greatly alarmed by their presence.

Meanwhile, Castagnier decided that he had lingered long enough. The tide had turned and at 10.00 p.m. on 20 February he ordered that his ships should weigh anchor and leave Lundy Roads.[7]

By now the breeze had freshened and Castagnier, cautious and concerned to the last, felt that the flood tide was not strong enough for him to make great headway. The fleet struggled on as far as Porlock, the wind strengthening by the minute. It was beginning to look as if time and tide were against them and Castagnier started to despair of ever making Bristol by daylight.

Another day in the Channel and the alarm would surely be given. And then the British would send God knows how many men-of-war to deal with the problem.

A hurried conference was held on the poop deck of the *Vengeance* with Castagnier suggesting that he might put the Legion ashore somewhere in Swansea Bay. Tate had his orders, however, and they were clear – if he could not make Bristol he should land in Cardigan Bay.[8] An argument ensued between Tate and Castagnier but Tate eventually carried the day. His instructions were explicit and that was something the Commodore could not deny.

As the fleet began to swing around, ready to sail back down the Bristol Channel, one of the prisoners from the Ilfracombe boats suddenly proved useful. Tyrell, in his later deposition, commented: 'Off Lundy they [we] took two small ships, out of which they [we] got a man who piloted the fleet into Cardigan Bay.'[9]

Whether the Ilfracombe sailor was a willing volunteer or whether he was pressed into service is not known. Whichever it might have been, his knowledge was extremely useful and saved Castagnier and his officers from spending hours poring over their charts.

At some stage in their journey, however – perhaps at the prompting of the Ilfracombe sailor, perhaps after careful study of the chart – Tate and Castagnier decided that the port of Fishguard would be their destination. It seemed to offer everything an invading force needed – a wide, open bay, gently shelving beaches, even a jetty or quay. What they did not know was whether or not the place was defended and that they could only find out when they arrived.

By 10.00 a.m. on 22 February, a fine and calm Wednesday morning, the French ships were off the Pembrokeshire coast. Yet again they had been recognised and identified, not as Russian ships but as French. At mid-morning Thomas Williams of Trelethin, himself an old sailor, spotted the four ships off the North Bishop Rock and was immediately suspicious.

Thomas Williams was now a magistrate and landowner and was nothing if not a practical man. An eyewitness account published some years later provides a vivid picture of Williams at this moment:

> At a little distance further along the cliff I espied the owner of Trelethin … standing very firm on his legs against a background of bright sea, his head inclining somewhat backwards, while with both his raised up hands he clutched a long spy glass, the small end of which was applied to his eye.[10]

It is easy to imagine the gathering of locals on the cliffs of Pembrokeshire, all of them eager to see something out of the ordinary:

> Following the direction of his spy glass, I perceived a yet more astounding sight – astonishing to us used to the world of lonely waters that lay stretched out in front of our homes. Three ships of war were passing slowly along our coast, not far from land; they were accompanied by a smaller craft which Mr Williams informed me was a lugger.[11]

By now the French fleet was flying British colours but Mr Williams was not taken in. It was customary at that time for captured vessels to be commissioned into service with the Royal Navy – as it was with any navy – and there is no doubt that many of the watchers that morning would have been aware of that fact. Therefore the clear French lines of the ships would not have deceived someone like Thomas Williams, not even for a moment – although it would have been unusual to find four captured French warships in one squadron, something that would have pushed credulity to the limits.

What did worry Williams was the simple fact that the four ships were sailing so close in shore, something that British ships would never have done. Then there was the fact that they were not following British naval routine and, most telling of all, their decks were crammed with soldiers.

'One of our squadrons, lost and off station,' someone ventured.

'A raiding party,' shouted somebody else. 'Could they be pirates, do you think?'

Thomas Williams shook his head and stared at his wife. She was an indomitable lady, as brave and formidable as her husband – and just as renowned. A local celebrity, only a few years before she had sailed out, single-handed, to rescue a party of shipwrecked sailors from the Bishop Rock, and Williams instinctively knew that she understood the situation perfectly.

'No,' she said now, 'not a lost squadron and certainly not pirates. This is invasion!'

Thomas Williams immediately sent a servant to raise the alarm at nearby Fishguard Fort, and then he and his wife – and a growing number of spectators – began to follow the ships around the coastline. It was, at times, a mad scramble, crawling over gullies and racing around headlands:

> Keeping the vessels in view, we followed them till nearly opposite the spot where they came to anchor, at two-o-clock, where they remained a considerable time in a state of inactivity.[12]

Castagnier and Tate could see the crowds upon the cliff tops and knew they had been recognised. They were astute enough to know that their false ensigns, Russian or British, would not fool old sailors for long – and there were bound to be at least a few old sailors up there on the cliffs.

Earlier in the morning off St David's Head they had encountered a small revenue cutter, the 'Diligence,' out from her base in Milford Haven on routine customs duties. The *Diligence* was a tiny 14-gun vessel, commanded by Lieutenant William Dobbin of the Royal Navy. She was no match for the heavily armed French ships which between them mounted nearly 120 guns of varying size and calibre. Her only recourse lay in flight.

Lieutenant Dobbin was a resourceful man, well-schooled in small boat tactics, and he quickly realised that his greatest weapon was the shallow draught of his ship. He ran for the shoal waters close to the cliffs of St David's Head where the larger French vessels were unable to follow. Castagnier, realising that he would be just wasting time waiting for the *Diligence* to re-emerge, left her and ploughed on towards Fishguard.

Once the French had gone, Dobbin sped back to Milford where he raised the alarm. Together with the other revenue officers from the *Speedwell* and seamen from his customs station he promptly joined the force which was beginning to form ready to march to the north and oppose the French, wherever they might decide to come ashore.

By 2.00 p.m., still watched by the ever vigilant Thomas Williams and his followers, the French ships had moored off Careg Wastad Point, a rocky headland on the Pencaer Peninsula. Careg Wastad Point lay two miles to the north west of Fishguard. The French had come to a halt and to Williams and his watchers they seemed to be in no hurry to move on.

* * *

Exactly what had Tate and Castagnier come to? The town and port of Fishguard was, to be sure, on the southern extremity of Cardigan Bay and to that extent at least Tate had obeyed his instructions from General Hoche. Compared to Bristol, however, Fishguard was tiny and lacking in substance. It was certainly a regional centre for trade but even within the remote world of West Wales places like Haverfordwest, Pembroke and Carmarthen were wealthier and more important towns.

In 1797 Fishguard had a population of just over 1,500. It was the third largest town in the county of Pembrokeshire (behind Pembroke and Haverfordwest) and in its own small way was quite a flourishing port. Despite its remote location, over a hundred miles from Cardiff and from the industrial heartland of Merthyr and the mining valleys, over fifty coastal vessels were based in the port. Most of these were engaged in the fishing industry but some operated as traders and as early forms of tramp vessels, hawking goods around the coast, selling to whoever needed their cargoes.

At this time there were two elements or parts to the town, the upper and lower sections. The upper part later became the central focus for the modern town while Lower Fishguard, situated along the eastern edge of the harbour and port, was perhaps the most populous.

Goodwick, two miles to the north west of Fishguard, was a straggling fishing village that seemed to be glued to the base of the Pencaer Peninsula. It was a separate community but very much part of the Fishguard environment and was where most of the fishermen of the region lived.

The whole area was dominated by the Pencaer Peninsula, a huge bulk of craggy rock that ran for a width of over twenty-five miles at its base and not much less at its tip. The area was wild and windswept, begrudgingly providing a living for those few men and women desperate enough to try and defeat the land.

Like a giant's fist, the Pencaer Peninsula thrust itself out into the rolling waters of Cardigan Bay. The famous railway engineer Isambard Kingdom Brunel was later to describe it as a barrier against the waves 'to prevent them separating the land from Fishguard'.[13] It was an accurate description, its presence creating in its lee the calm and sheltered lagoon of Fishguard Bay – outside the waves might be lashing at the coast; within the bay all would be calm and peaceful.

The men and women of Fishguard were used to the sea and ships. Timber, coal and lime were imported over the quay in the lower town while local produce such as slate, herring and grain were then loaded onto the ships for export to various parts of Wales and England. There was even a small shipbuilding industry located in the area close to the harbour.[14]

The term shipbuilding is probably a confusing one, maybe even misleading. The art of shipbuilding was then quite a simple process, vessels being constructed on slipways or even on the foreshore. Some fair degree of skill was required to actually produce the boats or ships but anyone with sufficient capital and enterprise could set himself up as a ship builder. At the end of the nineteenth century there were over thirty different locations around the Pembrokeshire coast where small wooden vessels were regularly being built. So ship building there might have been at Fishguard but it was not a particularly intricate or specialised trade.

Farming was hugely important to the area, often of the subsistence variety. On the larger farms – and there were some – labourers were hired for a year at a time. Wages were low, at best just a few pence a day, and meals thrown in, usually broth, bread and milk. For everyone, bartering was considered an essential part of life.

The role of women in this rural, almost peasant society was vital. To begin with it was crucial for women to bear male children to carry on the work of the farm. Equally as important, it was often far more convenient for the women of the house to deal with money matters, the hiring of labourers and so on. Men often worked on the land but many of them were also fishermen. It meant that they were either busy trying to hack out a living from the earth or were sometimes away from home for days, even weeks at a time.

Fishing was a difficult and dangerous trade in this part of west Wales. The weather was harsh, the sea nearly always wild. It was not uncommon for men to just disappear, sailing off and never returning from their travels.

At such times – and all too often it seemed – everything would be thrown back on the women. They kept house and they tilled the fields alongside or instead of their men. And, of course, it was not unusual for women to earn a little extra money by tasks such as spinning and weaving.[15] Jemima Nicholas, 47 years old at the time of the invasion, was one such woman. Powerful and well built – even if she was not the giant that legend was soon to declare – she sometimes earned extra money by working as the town cobbler.

Like all rural communities, Fishguard needed inland means of communication as well as sea-borne ones. Farmers needed to take goods for sale and while there was a flourishing market in Fishguard itself the desire for wider selling networks was always there.

A turnpike road connected the town to Haverfordwest, seventeen miles to the south and the largest, most significant market centre in the county. Heading northwards, a rough road led to Newport and Cardigan. Many miles beyond those two relatively small communities lay Aberystwyth, while the English border was 150 miles to the east, across rugged terrain with almost no recognisable roadways.

Despite its remoteness the area had already endured a brief brush or skirmish with warfare. On 15 September 1779, during the American War of Independence, Fishguard had been raided by the privateer *Black Prince*. Out from Dunkirk the privateer was sailing under American colours and was crewed by a mixed collection of Irish and English smugglers.

The town was bombarded and a ransom was demanded. A few houses were damaged and one or two people injured – one of them being Mary Fenton, sister of the Pembrokeshire historian Richard Fenton – but the ransom was refused. When a local smuggler decided to put to sea in his own small vessel and challenge the raider by returning fire it was too much for the crew of the *Black Prince*. There were easier pickings around the coast and the privateer promptly sailed away having achieved almost nothing.

For a long while local people believed that the privateer had been commanded by the famous John Paul Jones, the man later bestowed with the epithet 'Founder of the American Navy'. The legend was certainly not true but with Jones active around the Welsh and English coast at this time – at one stage he even landed on Caldey Island – it is easy to see how the story grew.

One thing that the *Black Prince* did achieve – hardly something she desired – was the creation of a fort at Fishguard. In the wake of the bombardment there had been an outcry in the town and local dignitaries decided to respond by building them a protective fort. Gwynne Vaughan of Jordanston gave the necessary piece of land, on Castle Point, a rocky headland just off the Cardigan/Newport Road. It was just over a mile distant from the town but it was blessed with a fine view of Fishguard Bay and the harbour.

The cost of building the fort was borne by Sir Hugh Owen of Orielton, a country estate and mansion house near Pembroke in the south of the county. Owen was, at that time, Lord Lieutenant of the region and took his responsibilities seriously, even down to paying for a defensive structure like Fishguard Fort.

The fort was really little more than a rigid gun platform and was later to be described as being just like a lady's fan in shape. However, it was better than nothing and its presence allowed the locals and the gentry of the county, people like Hugh Owen and Lord Milford, to sleep more soundly in their beds at night.

Building was complete by 1781 although the guns – permission to obtain and install such ordnance having to be gained from the Privy Council – were not fixed in place until 1785.[16] When the cannons were in position and all of the work complete Fishguard Fort was, potentially at least, a significant defensive work. Unfortunately, things were not always what they seemed.

The citadel was equipped with eight 9 pounder cannons. They were powerful enough weapons which dominated the inner reaches of the harbour but did not have a long enough range to cover the seaward approaches to the town. Goodwick Sands, the perfect landing site for any army and Pen Anglas Head, around which any invader would have to sail, were well beyond their range – something that Tate and his staff failed to appreciate.

Gwynne Vaughan, brother of the man who had barricaded himself into his house when news of the approaching French ships first broke, was appointed Governor of Fishguard Fort. The fort provided a base for the Fishguard Fencibles and the guns themselves were manned by three invalid gunners from Woolwich Arsenal.[17]

Finding enough ammunition for the guns was always a serious problem, something that could have had serious consequences during the invasion had things worked out differently. However, the mere presence of the fort and the deceptively efficient cannons did provide defence of a sort.

This, then, was the spot where Tate and Castagnier had chosen to come ashore. As the sun began to drop behind the bulk of Pencaer on 22 February the town of Fishguard was faced by a threat far greater than a mere privateer demanding ransom money. Now they would have to deal with an invading army.

In many respects Fishguard was an unlikely spot to create a revolution. It was remote and had little to recommend it as far as lines of communication were concerned. But Tate had at least reached his goal – which was a lot more than Generals Hoche and Quantin had ever managed to achieve. Now he had to do something about it.

Chapter 7

Tate's Landing

Having moored off Careg Wastad Point, Tate and Castagnier sat back to consider their next move. How – and where – to put the Legion ashore was the immediate problem. They had every reason to expect a reaction from the British, although the extent of that reaction was, as yet, not clear. Thomas Williams and his watchers from the cliff top may now have drifted away but Tate was sure they would have sent word to the authorities.

He was right about that. Mr Williams' servant had reported the presence of the French ships to the fort and, from there, a messenger was despatched to find Lieutenant Colonel Knox. As we have already seen, the commander of the local defence force was run to earth at Tregwynt House.

If the quality and quantity of the opposition were unknown, Tate must have realised that forces were already being marshalled against him and there was every reason to believe that the forces would be substantial. While things just then seemed quiet enough he knew it would not be long before he would be facing more than just a gathering of interested spectators. The most perilous part of their mission had just begun.

As if to prove the point, while he and Castagnier were debating their next move, the sudden cry of a lookout high above the deck broke across the still afternoon air. A ship was rapidly approaching the anchored fleet. Castagnier was furious that the ship had been able to come so close before being spotted but everyone's eyes had been on the shore, not on the sea behind them.

'A British frigate,' somebody called in alarm. 'They've run us down.'

Castagnier shook his head. 'No,' he said, reassuringly, 'not a frigate, not a warship at all. That's a merchant ship, a sloop. She's a coastal trader.'

As it turned out the new ship was the *Britannia*, bound for her home port of Fishguard and she was carrying a cargo of culm, intended for none other than Lieutenant Colonel Thomas Knox of the Fishguard Fencibles.

At Castagnier's command the *Vengeance* put a shot across the sloop's bows and the *Britannia* hove-to. A longboat was launched from the flagship and soon the master of the sloop, John Owen, was standing on the deck of the French frigate.

Owen was a local man, his house lying high up on the Pencaer Peninsula, and he knew instinctively that the French squadron posed a very real threat to the safety of the area. At first he refused to say anything but then, sitting in Castagnier's elegant stern cabin and sipping at a glass of good French brandy, he began to consider his options.

Owen was only too well aware of the real strength (or weakness) of the local defenders but he now decided that a game of bluff was called for. Asked about the size of the defending force in Fishguard, John Owen simply shrugged, took the actual number of Fishguard Fencibles, doubled it and gave an answer that felt right.

'I reckon there'll be 500 soldiers in the fort,' he told Castagnier, 'all well trained and armed – more than enough to take care of you.'

He sat back and gazed at the two French officers. They were fine looking men, he decided, and both of them seemed to have a good command of the English language.

'Where is this fort?' Tate asked.

Owen saw no reason to lie and, taking up the chart, pointed out the position of the defence work. Tate and Castagnier exchanged quick glances.

'I'll send in the *Vautour*,' Castagnier said and disappeared out of his cabin door. 'She will reconnoitre the harbour.'

The port and harbour lay just around the headland and Enseigne de Vaisseau Chosel, commander of the *Vautour*, knew that this was a mission of importance. He also knew it was a job that was fraught with danger. Nobody knew what might be waiting for them around the headland.

As the *Vautour* set off on her perilous journey, John Owen sat with the two French commanders, trying hard to discover their purpose. He had no idea of how many soldiers were on board the three ships – or their quality – but, with his practised eye, he reckoned well over 1,000.

The actual strength of the local Fencibles was thirteen officers, twelve sergeants, twelve drummers and fifers, and 285 part-time warriors – and that was if they all turned up for duty. His fictional estimate seemed a long way short of whatever men Tate had at his command.[1]

Meanwhile the *Vautour* had rounded Pen Anglas Head and surged into the broad expanse of Fishguard Bay. Almost immediately a cannon shot rang out. Nobody saw where the ball fell but Enseigne Chosel had no intention of staying to find out. Now thoroughly alarmed, he ordered his sailors to tack around, and in a swirl of foam the little lugger swept back to the comparative safety of the anchorage off Careg Wastad Point.

Within minutes Chosel was back alongside the flagship and was hurriedly reporting his news. Fishguard was defended – and defended with artillery. His report seemed to confirm what John Owen had told them, Tate thought. Castagnier agreed. The cannon shot told him that their true identity was now obviously known to everyone ashore and so he ordered the British ensign to be hauled down and the Republican tricolour run up in its place.

While Tate and Castagnier went into a hurried conference, John Owen had time to consider a curious incident which had occurred as he was brought on board the *Vengeance*. The moment his foot touched the quarterdeck he saw, among the French soldiers who were gathered together to watch proceedings, a man he recognised. It was a fellow Welshman, a fellow Fishguard resident in fact, by the name of James Bowen.

Until recently Bowen had been a servant at the farm of Trehowel up on the Peninsula. He had been almost a neighbour! The owner of

Trehowel, John Mortimer, had dismissed Bowen for horse stealing and Bowen had subsequently been wheeled into court and sentenced to transportation to Botany Bay. How he now came to be a member of the Legion Noire, Owen could not fathom. Possibly he had escaped or, more likely, his transporting prison ship had been captured by a privateer and Bowen had wound up in a French prison.

Such things did happen. The Irish officer Barry St Leger had found himself in exactly the same position, but it is unlikely that James Bowen would have been offered the choice of joining the Legion or waiting for repatriation, as had St Leger. His option would have been a matter of: 'You are joining the army – accept that fact or stay here and rot.'

Whatever the reason he had for being on board the *Vengeance*, James Bowen was clearly now a member of the Legion Noire. And when the time came it would be his local knowledge that led the French to their headquarters on the Pencaer Peninsula.

Tate and Castagnier were in something of a cleft stick. If Owen was right – and the experience of Enseigne Chosel on the *Vautour* appeared to back him up – there was no hope of landing in Fishguard. Any attempt to land against troops holding fixed defensive positions, troops that were backed up by artillery, would be to court disaster and all military thinking advised against it unless the situation was desperate.

Their present anchorage was a good one with plenty of deep water close inshore but they could not stay there indefinitely. That, too, would lead only to eventual discovery by the Royal Navy and the destruction of both the fleet and the Legion.

And so Tate and Castagnier made their decision. They would land the troops over the rocks here on Careg Wastad Point.

Before the landing took place there was one more thing that needed to be done. A cargo of culm was no use to the invaders and the *Britannia* was scuttled as she lay, rocking gently in the swell. John Owen was furious, seeing his livelihood disappearing under the waves but there was nothing he could do – for the moment at least.

After sinking the *Britannia* the landing began. Lord Cawdor was later to describe the moment with typical laconic ease. In his account of the affair he commented, succinctly, that on 22 February: 'Three ships of war and a lone lugger were observed off Fishguard but without creating any alarm until the Eve of that Day when they began to land men and were ascertained … to be French which created universal alarm.'[2]

Alarm was perhaps an understatement. The general interest and curiosity that had greeted the arrival of the French ships had been fuelled as much by ignorance as fear. Almost to the last, one observer continued to believe that the four vessels were nothing more sinister than a convoy of Liverpool merchantmen, becalmed and waiting for the tide to turn.[3]

However, following the appearance of the lugger *Vautour* at the entrance to the bay and the subsequent cannon shot from the fort, panic began to spread. The inhabitants of the farms on Pencaer, knowing that their lonely and exposed houses would be easy targets for the invaders, fled inland, taking refuge where and when they could find it.

One woman, Miss Ann Fenton – a relative of the Pembrokeshire historians and writers Richard and Ferrar Fenton – reportedly buried 800 guineas in gold under a hedge at the entrance to Fishguard's renowned beauty spot, the Gwaen Valley. Then, along with many of the other well-to-do people of the town, she fled. When she returned after the French surrender she immediately went to retrieve her money.

To the amazement of absolutely nobody, Ann Fenton found that her buried treasure had gone. Despite many searches and formal and informal treasure hunts the cache was never found. It is unlikely that such a sum – if it ever existed – had been taken by the French. Such wealth was beyond even the wildest dreams of the invaders and none of them would have been able to keep such bounty a secret. Presumably, then, some enterprising local character had watched Miss Fenton bury her money, seized his chance and made himself 800 guineas richer.[4]

The story is probably apocryphal but it does show the sense of panic that gripped the wealthy people of Fishguard and the surrounding countryside in the first few hours of the invasion. As Lord Cawdor said, there was 'universal alarm'.

Only the ordinary working people of the area remained stoical and unphased. They had nowhere to go and nothing of value to lose to the

French and so they gazed on the sight of their panic-stricken 'betters' with equanimity. Whether the invaders would win or be defeated was something over which they had no control or say. Whatever happened, the day-to-day life of the subsistence farmer or fisherman or labourer would not change very much. All they could do was to wait and see what would happen.

* * *

Once the decision to land on Careg Wastad Point was made things happened quickly. An advance party of twenty-five grenadiers, led by the young Irishman Barry St Leger, climbed into a longboat and pulled towards the rocks below the headland. They were the first men of the Legion Noire to come ashore.

The purpose of the advance party was twofold. Firstly, they were to secure the immediate area and create a landing point for the rest of the Legion. It was something that was easily achieved as there was no opposition. The second objective for St Leger and his grenadiers was to find and establish a house that would act as headquarters for William Tate.

As darkness fell, St Leger and his men scrambled up the 200ft cliff of Careg Wastad Point. It was a steep climb but it was cut by gullies and clefts in the rock and hillside. Even so, the soldiers, after almost a week on board ship, would have been gasping for breath by the time they reached the top of the cliff.

Once there St Leger did not stop but pushed on inland towards the farm house of Trehowel. Lying approximately a mile from the landing point, it is probable that the renegade Welshman and horse thief James Bowen either guided St Leger, or advised him on the location of Trehowel. St Leger did not mention Bowen in his later deposition and the matter remains one of conjecture but with an ex-servant of the house now serving with the Legion, the choice of Trehowel as headquarters would seem to have some relevance.[5]

John Mortimer, the tenant farmer from Trehowel, was about to be married and his house, where the wedding breakfast was going to be held, was well stocked with food and wine. By the time St Leger arrived at the house, Mortimer, like most of the other home owners on the Peninsula, had cleared out for safer pastures. The food and drink, however, were left behind.

Local legend declares that one of Mortimer's serving girls was in the process of drawing off a mug of beer for her master when news of the French ships was brought to the house. Mortimer immediately saddled his horse and left for the neighbouring farm of Llanwnwr at the foot of the Pencaer peninsula. The servants, he ordered, should get away as best they could.

The girl who was preparing the beer, rather than leave it for the French, followed in Mortimer's footsteps, carrying the mug with her. The story says that she arrived at Llanwnwr without having spilled a drop. The story might have little truth in it but one tale is definitely true – another servant carried away Mortimer's set of silver spoons and thus, almost certainly, saved them from plunder by the French.[6]

Arriving at Trehowel, St Leger found the place deserted and the door firmly bolted. He was inclined to try elsewhere but the grenadiers were in no mood for further physical activity. They may also have sensed an opportunity for plunder or, at least, a little foraging. Nobody answered to their knocks, but musket butts and booted feet soon battered a way in.

Ordering the grenadiers to remain in the courtyard, St Leger stepped gingerly inside the house. He took one look at the contents and knew that there was trouble ahead. As the grenadiers began to inch after him he pulled out his pistol and threatened to shoot the first man to cross the threshold. It was a bluff, but the grenadiers were old soldiers and the threats of a 20-year-old boy did not worry them unduly. They immediately trained their muskets on him.[7]

'Stand aside, Lieutenant,' one said. 'You've got one shot, we've got over twenty.'

St Leger lowered his pistol and the grenadiers swarmed into the house. The soldiers – and these were the cream of Tate's Legion, not the convicts or the chasseurs – had probably not drunk alcohol for some time; for the past few weeks they had been fed only basic ship's rations. Trehowel must have seemed like an Aladdin's Cave to them.

Within minutes the grenadiers were devouring all of the food and drink they could lay their hands on – and there was plenty of it. Distraught at their behaviour and at his inability to control his men, by his own admission St Leger later stated that he left the soldiers and wandered off.

In his deposition St Leger does not say why he left or where he went but it is easy to imagine the despair of the young and still idealistic officer. Possibly he intended to go back to the headland, find Tate and report what had happened. It was not long, however, before he began to have second thoughts. He had a duty to perform and so he decided to return to Trehowel and try to reassert his authority.

He found most of the grenadiers lying dead drunk in the house and garden, the liquor having gone straight to their heads. He also found some of them rolling around the courtyard and two of them about to 'set fire to the hay ricks which with difficulty he prevented.'[8]

How St Leger accomplished this feat is not known; probably by a combination of brute force with men too drunk to offer much resistance and by the lure of the brandy bottle. It took time but eventually he managed to subdue the men, who were soon snoring and oblivious.

The fear was always there, however, that they would sober up and start drinking again. Fortunately, as the night wore on, more officers and men from the Legion began to arrive at Trehowel to reinforce the advance party and establish the headquarters. St Leger was at last able to breathe easily again.

There had been almost no trouble getting ashore. The key word is 'almost'. St Leger had landed at approximately 5 p.m. and by 2 a.m. the following morning a further seventeen boatloads and equipment had followed him over the rocks onto Careg Wastad Point. It was not done without cost, however. One boat was lost, capsizing in the dark, and eight soldiers were drowned.

It is possible that this boat contained the artillery pieces for the Legion. Tate was an old artillery man and it is hard to imagine him setting off on an expedition like this without at least one cannon. None has ever been found, however, and there is no record of such weapons in the lists of captured ordnance compiled after the surrender.

The writer John Kinross has offered the explanation that artillery would have hampered rather than helped the Legion's march to Chester and Liverpool. And yet, according to Kinross, a sponson, or artillery sponge, was later found washed ashore, something that might well support the notion that there was a minimal amount of artillery with the Legion: 'A French cannon stands outside one of the Pencaer farmhouses today. It may well have been recovered from the sea.'[9]

To support his theory Kinross even adds to his book a photograph of the supposed French cannon outside Trenewydd farm house. The matter remains imponderable and the cannon is far more likely to have been one of the coastguard guns that were later carried behind the relieving force than a French weapon.

If there was no artillery the question has to be asked – why was a sponson later found washed up on the shores of the Peninsula? A small rowing boat made unstable by heavy cannon and ammunition could well have capsized but nobody has ever been able to find such items on the sea bed.

Tate had gone ashore early in the disembarkation and toiled up the slope with his men. Despite the fact that Trehowel had been secured and established as his HQ he chose to spend that first night on British soil with his troops on the cliff top. The master of the sunken sloop *Britannia*, John Owen, remained with him throughout the night.

Owen was concerned about Tate, an emotion that says much about the American's ability to charm both his friends and his enemies. Owen was later to write that: 'Tate had his bed and pillow spread on the ground. He had spent many nights like this, he said, and was happy to do it again.'[10]

Owen's concerns did not extend to putting his own life at risk. Early in the morning of 23 February, the first full day of the French presence and just as the rest of the Legion came ashore, he was granted permission to visit his family at Pontyago which lay a mile away. He wanted to check on their safety, he said, and promised to return within three hours. Perhaps wisely, he reneged on his promise and the French did not see him again.

After the accident and the drowning of eight soldiers, Tate had decided that it would be expedient to call a halt to the disembarkation, at least for the night. It meant that while the majority of the Legion Noire had been able to come ashore, there were still many soldiers on board the ships.

It is hard to know who got the better of the situation, the men on the clifftop or those still hunkered down in the holds of the ships. Those who were ashore either spent the rest of the night huddled around makeshift camp fires on the top of Careg Wastad Point or were corralled into the heavy and unwelcome task of manhandling supplies and ammunition up the cliff.

Long into the night the work parties toiled, their way lighted by clumps of gorse that had been set on fire. It must have been a terrifying sight for anyone who was watching or listening to the shouts and calls. At times it appeared as if the whole of the headland was alive and burning.

The soldiers worked on. By daybreak they had assembled an impressive arsenal – forty-seven barrels of gunpowder, twelve boxes of hand grenades, ten hampers and one sheet of ball cartridge. In addition, as daylight returned, disembarkation began again and there were now nearly 1,400 members of the Legion Noire surrounding the supply dump on the clifftop. They were armed with muskets, pistols and sabres.[10]

The Pencaer Peninsula was a rugged and barren stretch of land. It boasted several isolated farmhouses and the tiny village of Llanwnda with its equally tiny church but that was about it. Barely a hundred people lived on the Peninsula and the wind off the sea was normally as cold as an icicle.

The Legion Noire might not have been the cream of French military might, but they had achieved what many had thought of as an impossible dream. They were an enemy force, standing alone and at bay, on British soil.

Chapter 8

Defending the Nation

Had Tate and Castagnier realised, they could have walked ashore on that mild February afternoon in 1797 with next to no opposition and the whole county of Pembrokeshire lying open and available before them.

The only defenders that the town of Fishguard possessed were its part-time Fencibles and even these enthusiastic but decidedly amateur and ill-trained volunteers needed time to assemble at the town fort. Many of them toiled in the fields on a daily basis, others on the fishing boats; it would have been several hours before anything like a viable complement was assembled.

As Enseigne Chosel had found out when he sailed into the bay, Fishguard Fort was, at least, ready and prepared with its Woolwich gunners alert and eager to fight. There was one slight problem, however – the shot they had fired had been a blank. Had the men on the *Vautour* been a little more adventurous and decided to stand in close to the fort and open fire they would have made short work indeed of Fishguard's defences.[1]

In the days after the surrender Gwynne Vaughan, Governor of the town's citadel, wrote to the Duke of Portland, the Home Secretary, describing the landing and the subsequent departure of Castagnier's ships. Almost as an aside he happened to mention the lack of shot and shell in the fort:

I beg leave to remark to Your Grace that had these ships moored in Fishguard Bay, both the Fort and the town of Fishguard would have been battered to pieces, I having but three rounds of ammunition for my guns (being eight Nine

Pounders) to oppose them. I therefore hope Your Grace will judge it proper to order some powder for this service as soon as possible.[2]

There has been debate about the fort's blank shot. Was it a deliberate ruse or were the gunners firing a salute to the British colours that the lugger was, at that time, still flying? In some quarters the shot has been seen simply as an alarm for the local community: 'The so-called salute to the British colours was the firing of the alarm gun to summon the local Volunteer force.'[3]

All of the suggestions have a degree of credibility. However, by the time the *Vautour* entered Fishguard Bay the messenger from Mr Williams of Trelethin would have arrived with the news, the terrifying news, that the ships off the coast were French and that, clearly, they intended to effect a landing or begin a bombardment of the town. Knowing the true nationality of the *Vautour* and sensing her purpose it would have been highly unlikely that the gunners would have fired a welcoming salute.

Similarly, with the French ships now here before them, the gunners would not have opened fire just to call in the Fencibles. The message to assemble had already gone out and it would, by then, have been too late; the enemy was already upon them.

The firing of the cannon was, in all probability, a desperate ruse by Ensign Bowen, the only officer then on duty in the fort, with the intention of deterring the French ship from making further progress into the harbour. If the *Vautour* had pushed on the chances are that one of the live charges would have been used – with ammunition so low it would have been important to preserve it for as long as possible.

This view is supported by the words of Peter Davies, one of the volunteer artillerymen who assisted the Woolwich gunners. Davies, a typically stoic north Pembrokeshire countryman, normally earned his living as a tailor in the town but on this day he was proud to regard himself as one of Fishguard's defenders. Ferrar Fenton has written: 'I can remember Peter Davies as an old man, very proud of his part in the action, and that he had been captain of a gun in it. 'We did fight famoos [sic],' he used to say, 'and the French did run away, and we did fire after them."[4]

Whatever the reasons behind firing the shot, it certainly misled the French into believing that the cannon in the fort were efficiently handled and well supplied with ammunition. As a consequence, the *Vautour* fled the harbour and Tate was forced to land his troops over the slippery rocks of Careg Wastad Point.

He was lucky that it was such a fine evening. If the sea had been anything other than mill-pond calm the boats would have been dashed against the rocks and disaster would have overwhelmed them.

* * *

Having been summoned from his dinner and dance at Tregwynt, Lieutenant Colonel Thomas Knox, the commander of Fishguard's only real defence, hurried towards his command post at the fort. If the ships were French – and he was still not sure about that – their behaviour was more than a little perplexing. He was curious and puzzled why the commander had moored off Careg Wastad Point and was not sending troops ashore into the town or onto nearby Goodwick Sands.

Knox took the coastal road back to Fishguard and at several vantage points during the journey he was able to stop and gaze out towards the vessels still moored off the headland. He may have recognised the *Britannia*. He certainly knew her, and her Master John Owen. Only a day or so before, he had supervised her loading down on the Cleddau River. Her presence alongside the other ships would have confused him even more; perhaps it was, after all, just a mistake.

On the other hand, the groups of fleeing householders that he met as he rode towards town all assured him that the new arrivals were French and that they were now coming ashore. Even at this early stage Knox knew that he had to have more information.

Riding hard across Goodwick Sands, Knox met Ensign Bowen and seventy of the Fencibles who had reported eagerly to the fort, ready for duty, as soon as the alarm had been given. They were now marching out to meet the enemy. Accompanying them was a retired, half-pay officer called Thomas Nesbitt who was in Fishguard waiting for a ship to take him to Ireland.

On hearing of the French ships, Nesbitt had immediately come forward to volunteer his services, an offer which was eagerly accepted. At Knox's suggestion he now selected and took charge of a team of scouts, men who knew the area and were not frightened to shadow enemy troops. After a few brief courtesies, he wished Knox good day and set off to gather the information that the Lieutenant Colonel needed. In the meantime, Knox led the rest of his men back to Fishguard Fort.

The Fencibles were, understandably, aggrieved. Their blood was up and they wanted to come face to face with an enemy that had had the nerve to land in their back yard. However, with dusk settling across the Peninsula, Knox felt that to attack with such a small force would be a mistake that could lead to unpleasant consequences for all concerned.

In hindsight, Knox's decision was the wrong one. A determined attack on the French as they scrambled out of their boats and up the cliffs of Careg Wastad would probably have driven away the interlopers before they had even gained a foothold. But at this stage he did not know his enemy and a reverse up on the slopes of the Peninsula would have left Fishguard wide open and vulnerable. For all he knew he could be walking into an ambush and so, despite the grumbling of his men, he decided that discretion was the better part of valour.

Once he arrived at the fort, Knox considered his options. His Fencibles were made up of two sections, his own at Fishguard and that of Major Bowen at Newport. Knox now ordered the firing of a cannon (a blank charge, yet again) to alert Major Bowen at Llwyngwair where the Newport Division of the Fencibles was based. He followed this up with a letter asking the Major to mobilise his Division and bring them to the nearby village of Dinas.

Not yet knowing the enemy strength, it was a sensible decision. If the French were there in numbers, Knox would need Bowen's troops to cover a withdrawal. If he wanted them to join him in an attack, they could be quickly summoned.

And then Knox changed his mind. Beset by indecision, he ordered Bowen's forces to come directly to Fishguard and join him in the fort.

His change of heart may have been due to the arrival at the citadel of a local man by the name of Thomas Williams. It was now nearly 8.30 p.m. and pitch dark. Williams claimed to have been taken prisoner by twelve French soldiers. He was wounded in the scuffle, he said, but somehow he had managed to slip away in the darkness.

Knox, who had until now retained an air of scepticism, or at best, a sort of patrician disdain that he and his father had perfected, examined Williams' wounds and became immediately convinced that he was facing overwhelming odds. The French were clearly ashore. He sent an immediate message to Lord Milford, the Lord Lieutenant at Picton Castle, informing him of the state of affairs, and sat down to consider his options. He quickly came to the conclusion that there was no alternative – he would attack the French at first light.

* * *

At the end of the nineteenth century the Fishguard Fencibles were just one small cog in the defence system of Britain. The regular army was a relatively small force, spread thinly across the globe, and played virtually no part in defending the homeland.

Mass conscription had been introduced in France back in 1793 and the British government would have dearly loved to implement a similar scheme in the United Kingdom, but Prime Minister William Pitt knew he did not dare to create such an innovatory and creative practice. Public opinion would have howled him down.

The British people were proud of their naval heritage and tolerated the press gang as a necessary evil; they were much less supportive of the army, believing that the ranks of the various regiments were little better than safe havens for the scum of the prisons. They were not prepared to invest the army with powers that were broadly similar to those of the navy and, as a result, the government was forced to fall back on other measures.[5]

The regular army, it was decided, would continue to wage war abroad. Land defence of Britain consequently rested on the shoulders of two separate bodies, the militia and the various volunteer regiments that had been founded in most coastal areas of the country.

While the government stopped short of conscription, militia service had been made compulsory for all able bodied men in 1757, in theory at least creating a huge pool of trained semi-professional soldiers who would be available for service when required. The process worked reasonably well. In peacetime men were called up for training with the militia and once they had achieved a desired standard they were allowed to return to their homes and jobs. There was nothing particularly onerous about that.

However, in times of war, militia men were retained as a standing army and were then liable to be sent anywhere in Britain. By the terms of Lord Strange's Bill of 1769, each county in England, Scotland and Wales was required to raise its own militia regiment for the defence of the country and faced heavy fines if they failed to comply. As a result, by 1794 a force of over 6,000 cavalry and 5,000 infantry had been raised. The Supplementary Militia Bill of 1796 saw the figure extended by many thousands.[6]

The Pembrokeshire Militia had been formed in 1780. Their commander was Colonel John Colby of Ffynone. Aged 46 when the invasion took place, Colby was a capable and experienced officer, although his real interests were in business and land management, not the control or direction of the militia – for which he really had very little time.

Militia men undoubtedly had certain privileges. Each man was granted parish relief and the uniforms that the soldiers wore were invariably colourful and exotic – something that certainly attracted the young ladies! A bounty of six pence, a significant sum in those days, was paid on enlistment and with the regiment liable to be sent anywhere in the country, the traditional limitations imposed by geographical immobility were being broken down.

For young men with no ties militia service could be an interesting and mind-broadening experience. While the militia would not be sent overseas, simply to serve, as the Pembrokeshire Militia did, in places such as Felixstowe where they occupied Landguard Fort, was like having a brief taste of paradise. Sometimes the postings were a lot closer to home, however. In 1797 the Cardigan Militia found itself in no less a place than Pembrokeshire where, under Lieutenant Cole, they acted as guards for captured French prisoners.

Militia officers had a particularly pleasant time. They enjoyed an active social life with balls, dinners and hunt meets being the regular order of the day – all without any real fear of conflict. Even just promenading up and down town or village streets was an occupation that pleased everyone, officers and locals alike. Jane Austen's picture of a militia regiment arriving in the home town of Lizzie and Jane Bennett in *Pride and Prejudice* is undoubtedly an accurate one:

> The attention of the younger ones was then no longer to be gained by him. Their eyes were immediately wandering up the street in quest of the officers, and nothing less than a very smart bonnet indeed, or a really new muslin in a shop window, could recall them.[7]

However, there were also drawbacks to militia service. Selection was by means of a ballot among those eligible for service – it would not do to have every single working man in the country signed up as a soldier – and after five years a second ballot was held in order to provide replacements. This meant that trained and experienced soldiers were invariably lost after just a few years before the colours.

Service in the militia was not universally popular. For one thing the militia could be used as peacekeepers and that might mean taking up arms against people with whom the militia men had a degree of sympathy – one of the reasons why, in time of war, they were sent to serve well away from their home locations.

Perhaps most invidious of all, any man could avoid service if he so chose, usually either by paying a fine or by finding a substitute.[8]

In times of war finding substitutes was no easy matter and so the payment of a fine became the standard way of avoiding militia service. Handing across money might have worked miracles for the revenue budget of a regiment but it did little to increase the fighting force. It meant that until the final years of the nineteenth century (when the

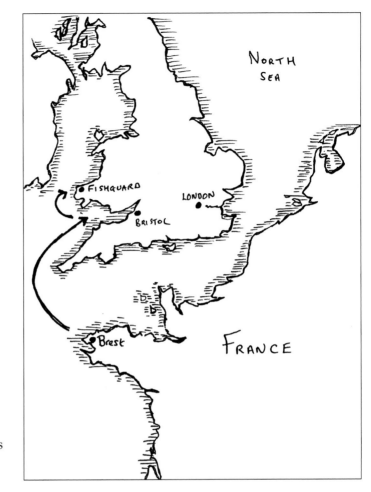

Right: The invasion route, from Brest to Fishguard. (1797)

Below: Looking towards Fishguard, the view from Fishguard Fort.

Above: A pen and ink drawing of Tregwynt where Colonel Knox heard the news of the French landing.

Below: Pencaer Peninsula, the invasion area.

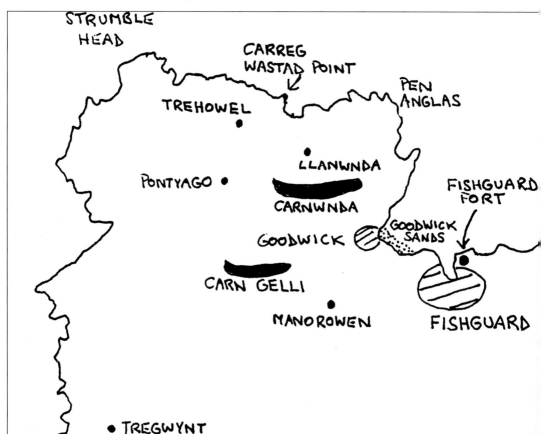

Above: Fishguard Fort sits on the headland.

Below: Lower Fishguard and the town ship building area.

Left: A Fishguard Fencible, from an early print. *c.* 1797.

Below: The city and cathedral of St David's – the cathedral lost the lead from its roof during the invasion scare.

Above: Fishguard Bay.

Below: Pickton Castle, home of Lord Milford.

Left: Trefgarne Rocks where the British forces met.

Below: Carnwndda Rocks with the village of Llanwnda in the foreground.

A composite postcard showing locations in the story, produced for the centenary of the invasion in 1897.

Above: Trehowel Farmhouse, looking dark and mysterious.

Below: French troops coming ashore on Careg Wastad Point, a contemporary image.

The village of Goodwick.

Looking to the south, the view from Careg Wastad Point.

Another view from Careg Wastad.

Above: The square at Fishguard.

Below: Llanwnda Church, ransacked and despoiled by the invading French.

The Royal Oak, where the surrender took place – not a pub in those days but a simple town house.

Left: Trehowel Farm House, the French headquarters.

Below: Goodwick Beach where the surrendering French lined up ready to be marched into captivity.

Above: A contemporary print showing the French in the process of surrendering – not entirely accurate but certainly atmospheric.

Right: The memorial stone on Careg Wastad point, erected in 1897.

A contemporary painting of the surrender, primitive in style and probably painted in the months after the event.

A Welsh woman in traditional costume – did the women and their dress play a part in the defeat of the French?

Above: The capture of Resistance, one of the French fleet.

Below: The invasion attempt on Ireland failed in 1796 – this contemporary print gives a dramatic interpretation of the storm that ended it all.

Above left: Lord Cawdor, the undoubted hero of the hour.

Above right: Lazarre Hoche, the young but dying general who masterminded the invasion.

Robespierre, evil genius of the French revolution.

THEOBALD WOLFE TONE.

From a Portrait by his Daughter-in-law, Mrs. Sampson Tone.

Above left: Wolfe Tone played a peripheral role in the invasion of Fishguard but still a man much feared by the British.

Above right: Lafayette, hero and adventurer, shown here in prison.

The Bible from Llanwnda Church, torn and despoiled during the invasion period.

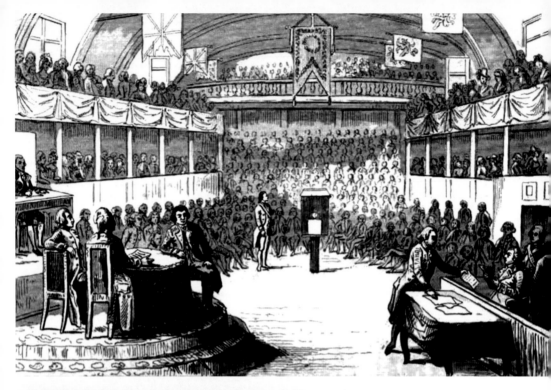

Above: The trial of King Louis.

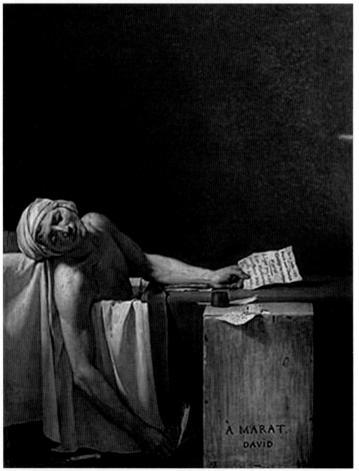

Left: David's famous painting of the death of journalist and rabble rouser Marat.

Supplementary Militia Bill came into force), almost all of the militia regiments in the country were woefully undermanned.

By pure chance, the commander of the Pembrokeshire Militia was at home in the county during the early part of 1797. John Colby had returned from Felixstowe to train extra militia men who had recently been recruited and was actually at his town house in Haverfordwest when news of the French landing broke. It was a lucky coincidence for the defenders of the county – to have an experienced local commander able to serve during a crisis was very far from normal.

So much for the militia – the volunteer units were a rather different matter. If the militias were generally regarded as efficient and well trained, the volunteers were purely local defence forces, interested only in their own specific regions and in existence only in times of armed conflict. They were a cheap and decidedly homespun group and therefore weapons such as artillery were rarely considered appropriate or necessary.

The guns at Fishguard Fort were an exception rather than a rule and possession of such weapons usually came down to the amount of influence local dignitaries could wield or, sometimes, to the amount of money they were prepared to distribute.

The volunteer infantry units were known as Fencibles, even though the term was supposed to apply only to regular soldiers who had enlisted for home service in times of war. The term covered retired or infirm warriors like the Woolwich gunners at Fishguard Fort.

Weapons were usually supplied by the government but resources were limited and many men were forced to parade armed with bill hooks, scythes and sticks pulled from the hedgerow. The result was usually a ragbag collection of men that might terrify the old ladies of the town but was highly unlikely to cause much alarm to the enemy.

An amusing description of a Fencible unit can be found in John Whiting's play *A Penny for a Song*. Set in England during the later invasion-scare period of 1804, the appearance of the Fencibles and the attitude of the general public towards these well-meaning amateurs have a ring of truth about them. Impressions and attitudes, not to mention performance, would not have been much different in 1797. Here, Sir Timothy Bellboys is describing to a visitor the local defence force: 'If you should chance upon a ragged band of scruffy, drunken, ill disciplined, noisy louts rampaging the countryside you will be viewing our sole defence.'9

Only a little later in the play, when the Fencibles appear on stage for the first time, they are poorly armed with broom sticks and scythes and there is not one scrap of uniformity about their appearance. The unit comprises farm labourers, tradesmen – even the local vicar.

The Fishguard Fencibles were the brain child of William Knox who served as the Under Secretary of State for America from 1770 until the post was abolished in 1782 after the cessation of the Colonies. On his retirement, William Knox bought large estates at Llanstinan and Slebech in Pembrokeshire and was, in the 1790s, still a newcomer to the county and its upper-class society.

He was haughty and self-opinionated; an undoubtedly brilliant man but one who was difficult to relate to and like. He had refused a knighthood because he felt that he deserved a baronetcy. It was a typical Knox response to what he felt was an insult. He was disliked by all his neighbours and by most of the 'establishment' of the county and that dislike rubbed off onto his family.

When war broke out with Republican France in 1793 Knox immediately offered to raise a full regiment of volunteer troops – more importantly, he offered to do it at his own expense. It was a magnanimous gesture, one that the government eagerly seized. Unfortunately, he rather spoiled the moment by installing his son Thomas as commander of the unit.

Within two years the Fishguard Fencibles were established after being approved by government. Approval was important as since the days of Henry Tudor nobody could simply raise a private army when and where he liked. The members of the Fencibles were, in the main, farmers and tradesmen but Knox Junior reigned over them with haughty disdain. He bore the rank of Lieutenant Colonel.

Thomas Knox had achieved a rapid, almost miraculous promotion, one that was equalled only by the new young generals of the French

Republic. The difference between men like Hoche, Napoleon and young Knox was that the Frenchmen had achieved their rank by proving themselves on the field of battle. Knox had, so far, never heard a shot fired in anger.[10]

The Fishguard Fencibles wore a distinctive uniform – a striped jacket, white or light coloured breeches and a slouch hat with the motto 'Ich Dien' pinned to the side. They were divided into two sections, one under Thomas Knox and based at Fishguard Fort, and the other under Major Bowen, based in nearby Llwyngwair outside Newport.

The nominal strength may have been 285 men but it was only rarely that the full complement presented itself for parade. A return showing the forces gathered to oppose the French invaders lists only 190 non-commissioned officers and men of the Fencibles as present on 23 and 24 February, when the invasion scare was at its height.[11]

There were no records explaining absences but many of the men would have been detained elsewhere – most likely at sea or away selling produce. In the case of Colonel Daniel Vaughan – who we last saw leaving Mrs Harries' dinner party at Tregwynt – he was too ill to present himself at the fort. Commissioned as one of Knox's officers, Vaughan was old and infirm and would have been a liability on the battlefield. He did not shirk his duties, however, as his determined barricading of his house clearly demonstrated.

It is perhaps uncharitable, but the thought of imminent bloodshed may have proved too frightening a prospect for some of the Fencibles. It was fine to parade and charge around the countryside on manoeuvres – like John Whiting's Bellboys Fencibles – but to actually risk being maimed or killed in a fire fight was a totally different matter.

Joining a volunteer unit like the Fishguard Fencibles was another way of avoiding militia service, as enlisting as a volunteer offered immediate exemption. To many it would have been a very passable alternative. Nobody had ever expected to have to fight, that was something best left to the militia. But now, suddenly, the French were here and blood and battle lay just over the headland.

The Fishguard Fencibles were not the only volunteer unit in Pembrokeshire at the time of the invasion but the Pembroke Fencibles, sometimes known as the Pembroke Volunteers, was the only other infantry unit. Commanded by Major James Ackland, Lieutenant Lord and Ensign Ridgway, ninety-three men from the Pembroke Volunteers marched to Fishguard with Lord Cawdor to add their weight to the strength of the defenders.[12] Like their counterparts in the north of the county they were willing and enthusiastic but, at the end of the day, they were only farmers and tradesmen who were willing 'to have a go'.

In addition to the two infantry units there were also two troops of Gentlemen and Yeomanry Cavalry. They had been in existence for three years, since 19 April 1794. Then, in response to a government request to raise bodies of cavalry in each of the counties, the important gentlemen in Pembrokeshire society decided to do something about the government's plea.

On that day a meeting was convened and chaired by Lord Milford. It was held in London where the gentlemen of the county were enjoying the season. At the meeting it was agreed to raise the two troops of yeomen cavalry, the men being: 'Exempt from the Militia Ballot and Horse Duty. They were to provide their own horses, the government their arms and accoutrements.'[13]

The two troops were named after the Hundreds in which they were raised and stationed. They were the Dungleddy Troop, commanded by Lord Milford, and the Castlemartin Troop under Lord Cawdor of Stackpole Court. Hundreds were archaic administrative areas established after the Acts of Union between England and Wales in the 1530s, but at that time still used for things like magistrates' courts and other minor aspects of local government.

Dungleddy was the land set between the two arms of the Cleddau River, consisting mainly of land around Lord Milford's seat at Picton Castle and Haverfordwest. The name derives from the Welsh word Daugleddy – in English, more or less 'the two Cleddau'. Castlemartin Hundred covered the area between Milford Haven and the south Pembrokeshire coast, including Lord Cawdor's estates at Stackpole.

Each troop was made up of fifty men, armed with swords, pistols and carbines. Their uniforms were varied but, in the main, consisted of white breeches, blue coats with buff collars and lapels, and a leather helmet. The helmet was covered with a moleskin turban and a bearskin crest.[14] Troopers were allowed to claim pay when they were on exercise or duty – a privilege not extended to the wealthier officers who were to receive remuneration only when on active service.

Despite the disparities in pay, the fact that troopers and officers had to provide their own horses seems to indicate that only those who were substantially well off would have been able to join these cavalry troops. They were effectively the elite of volunteer regiments and those not able to afford the horse would have to content themselves with the more humble infantry Fencibles.

This, then, was the size and state of the defenders within the county of Pembrokeshire in February 1797. Sailors on various ships moored in Milford Haven and the redoubtable revenue men who had already encountered the French, might add a few more. But it was still a tiny force and on paper at least it should have been a no-contest.

* * *

There can be no doubt that as Knox settled down for an uncomfortable and sleepless night in Fishguard Fort his mind would have been whirling. There was so much to think about. Above all he would have pondered on the men he could count on to help him in the defence of the town. His own forces were pitifully few but he wondered what would Lord Milford do? Who would he send to help? Would he send anyone? And how soon would they get there?

At this stage Lieutenant Colonel Thomas Knox had little doubt that he was the man most qualified to command the defending force. He was, after all, in place at Fishguard. He knew the terrain and he had the rank. He was his father's son and his ego would not allow him to consider that anyone might even dream of superseding his authority.

No doubt, as he sat there or paced the floor, he would have counted the numbers and quality of the troops available within the county. His calculations would not have been reassuring. Whichever way he looked at it, he doubted that any reinforcements would number more than a couple of hundred. He desperately needed information from

Thomas Nesbitt and his scouts but, as yet, there was no sign of the half-pay officer who had so willingly offered his services. It was hardly charitable, but Knox was puzzled by the lack of news from the Pencaer Peninsula.

'Damn it all!' he muttered to himself as he gazed for the twentieth or thirtieth time across the harbour to the heights of Pencaer and Careg Wastad. 'Where are you Nesbitt? Have you run away like the rest of them? I need to know how many French there are.'

The night had grown darker than ever and the lack of wind made everything seem deathless and still. Knox, like most north Pembrokeshire people, was not used to such silence and there can be no doubt that it unnerved him a little.

Knox had told Lord Milford in his letter that he intended to attack at dawn. Now, in the long reaches of the night, he began to have second thoughts.

Chapter 9

Establishing the Beachhead

During their first night ashore, the soldiers of the Legion Noire made short work of the livestock from Trehowel, Pontyago and other isolated farm houses on the Peninsula. Even the wildlife of the region, everything from rabbits and hares to seagulls and pigeons, was swiftly caught and eaten, either raw or half-cooked over the camp fires.

One group of starving men simply purloined the butter from a dairy attached to a farm house. They melted the butter in a large pot over a camp fire and cooked chickens, feathers and gizzards included, in that.

The effect of half cooked and rich, butter-seasoned food on empty bellies can be imagined. The French had brought few provisions, a little cheese and biscuits, but by tapping some of the barrels of brandy that had been intended to induce the populace to join them, the soldiers were at least able to keep warm. But brandy, butter and raw chicken can be a lethal combination, as many of the soldiers soon found out.

Having established the Legion headquarters at Trehowel, Barry St Leger was not allowed to rest on his laurels. He was soon instructed to take another party of grenadiers and occupy the heights of nearby Carnwndda. The rocky hill stood 500ft in height and dominated not only the village of Llanwnda but also the surrounding countryside and the approaches to Careg Wastad Point.

Llanwnda was a tiny settlement, just a few houses and a church. It barely deserved the epithet hamlet, let alone village. Carnwndda, just 100 yards to the south, was a natural fortress, able to be comfortably climbed only from the seaward side. Here Barry St Leger established his picket and settled down to await developments.

St Leger and his grenadiers, supposedly the best disciplined part of the invasion force, were in command of the most important strategic position on the Peninsula. With the rest of the Legion Noire either ashore or in the process of landing, at this moment it would have taken a very determined assault to dislodge the invaders.

When morning came it brought swift and sudden movement. A large contingent of French soldiers left the encampment on the clifftop and marched inland. They passed the headquarters at Trehowel and moved on towards Pontyago, the home of Captain John Owen. Here they paused briefly and then split into two groups.

The first group moved off to establish itself at the south-west tip of Carnwndda, a section of the hill called Carn Gelli. The second group began clambering over the rocks of Carnwndda itself until, reaching the summit, they reinforced St Leger's overnight picket. The French were now established along the line of high rocks from Carnwndda in the north to Carn Gelli in the south. If St Leger's position had been strong, the reinforcements made it even stronger.

So far, the dispositions and the management of the troops had been exemplary. Any British attack on the French would have to pass these two rocky outcrops. The grenadiers, possibly over 600 of them, were well dug in and their black uniforms blended easily with the dark background. They commanded the high ground and for the moment at least seemed to be in total control.

On the heights of Carnwndda the French solemnly raised the tricolour. It snapped out and billowed in the morning breeze as the soldiers began fortifying their position.

Two forward pickets were thrown out, one from Carn Gelli and from Carnwndda itself. Observers were soon able to pick out a French officer who made regular forays into the open countryside, waving a large French flag. His purpose seemed to be to encourage any watching locals in the immediate vicinity to come forward and join the Legion.

Observers may have been few and far between that morning but the idea was not necessarily a bad one, at least not in the eyes of the French commanders.

* * *

Wales was always intended as a 'happy hunting ground' for Tate and his Legion. The original plan, once the town and port of Bristol was sacked, had been for them to cross over the Severn Estuary. There had never been any intention of operations in the south west of England, but in Wales they were to cause mayhem in the inland counties as they marched towards Liverpool and Chester. Tate's orders were clear – Wales was not just an area to march through; it was as much a target as Liverpool.

The reason for this specific order was clear. Wales was a country which everyone in the Directory assumed – and genuinely believed – was a hotbed of rebellion and revolt. It needed to be exposed to the French war machine and if its people could not be persuaded to join the marching Legion then they would have to face the consequences. Either way Tate's activities in Wales would teach the perfidious British a lesson.

The reasons for this belief are relatively easy to see and appreciate. From the moment the Bastille fell, a tide of republicanism had swept through Europe and France had felt the influence of some of the most influential radicals of the day. By pure chance a large number of those radicals just happened to be Welsh.

Dr Richard Price, a Welshman who had lived almost all his adult life in London, and John Jones, the author of *A Star under a Cloud*, a man commonly regarded as a disciple of Tom Paine, had both been vocal in their support of the revolution. Thomas Evans, better known as Tomos Glyn Cothi, had been one of the editors of radical journal *The Welsh Repository* and was put in the public pillory at Carmarthen after performing what was regarded as a seditious song.

Support from such men had been essential for the new Republic, even if it consisted in the main of mere words and sentiments. When words transformed into deeds, however, they were eagerly grasped by the besieged revolutionaries. The assistance of David Williams, a personal friend of the Girodin Jacques-Pierre Brissot, was considered a significant event. Williams crossed over to France in order to demonstrate his solidarity with the revolution and, like Tom Paine, in 1792 he was made a French citizen.

The Baptist minister Morgan John Rhys was another Welsh radical who went to France, in his case to distribute Bibles. Iolo Morganwg, the self-styled 'enemy of kings' (though not, he was quick to add, of British kings) was another whose name and voice were constantly heard in the new Republic. Iolo Morganwg and all of the others; their influence was felt long before Wolfe Tone and the United Irishmen appeared on the scene and the country of their birth and origin was not lost on the French leaders.

Unfortunately for the Welsh radicals, their belief in the ideals of the French Revolution was short lived. It was soon shattered by the Terror and by the excesses of Robespierre and the Jacobins. The Welsh radicals were thinkers, men of ideas who were made for discussion around the tavern fire or in the coffee shop. They were not, in the main, men of action.

For many of the radicals, the Terror placed them in an invidious position; they could not condone what was happening in France but they had burned their bridges behind them. Morgan John Rhys, in particular, found serious disfavour in the eyes of William Pitt who considered him a dangerous Jacobin.

As the excesses of the Terror gathered momentum, most of the Welsh radicals either gave up supporting the French revolt or attempted to 'lie low'. Some like Rhys, sought refuge in countries such as America.

Yet despite the decidedly malleable views of the Welsh intelligentsia, in some respects the Directory was not totally misguided or in the wrong about the situation in Wales. It was in the matter of degree that they made their mistake.

During the last decade of the eighteenth century there was a significant amount of unrest in the countryside, as there was in many other parts of Britain. Low prices for the sale of corn and grain as well as poor harvests and exploitative landowners all contributed to a simmering resentment that bubbled under the surface.

Just two years before the invasion there had been bread riots in Haverfordwest, riots that resulted in the militia being called out. The same year there was a much more serious disturbance when miners from Hook brought chaos and confusion to the county town and the Riot Act had to be read. The riots were unpleasant and unsettling but in the main they were uprisings that were directed at poor living conditions rather than anything else.

In an age where a farm labourer's daily ration of food was based on barley bread and a little milk, where meat was probably taken as rarely as once a month, some disquiet might have been expected. It did not mean that the people were ever likely, at least in the immediate future, to rise up against the government – local landowners yes, Westminster no.

Despite this the Directory may well have been right in thinking that it needed only a trigger for the Welsh to rise up in open rebellion. They had done it before, many times, but the result of all the rebellions against the English crown and government, from Llewellyn the Last through to Owain Glyndwr, had always ended in one way – defeat for the Welsh.

As a nation, the Welsh were certainly not cowed but it would have to be a very significant and compelling trigger to make the Welsh take up arms again. And unfortunately the Legion Noire was neither significant nor compelling.

If, at the end of the eighteenth century Wales was not the hot bed of revolt and rebellion that the Directory believed it to be, it certainly had capabilities, as Capability Brown might have said. One thing was clear however: as far as religion was concerned the country was certainly a hotbed of Dissenters.

The established church was in a state of decay and absentee Bishops were common. When appointments were made it was rare for the new Bishop to be a Welshman. In fact, in the hundred years between 1700 and 1800, only three out of sixty-two appointments to Bishoprics were Welshmen.[2] There was a great sense of religious dissatisfaction, at all levels, within the country. And into the vacuum that was created by a largely ineffective and absent church stepped the Nonconformists.

A sense of imposition seemed to have settled over Welsh spiritual affairs. The Anglican Church, cloak it or cover it how you like, was thought of as an English body where, with the Bishops being unable to understand either the Welsh language or the Welsh people, there was a sense of alienation in the air. It needed strong and dynamic leadership if the church was going to thrive but this was sadly lacking. Such a state of affairs did not mean that there was any lack of interest in religion or, perhaps more importantly, in the concept of saving one's soul. In fact it was just the opposite.

The great spiritual reawakening that was taking place in Wales during the eighteenth century simply added to the sense of turmoil, and for those looking at the situation from a distance – such as the Directory in Republican France – it really did seem as if the country was about to explode. It was, as Robespierre might have said, fertile ground for a revolution.

The religious debate was fuelled by the preaching, usually in the open air, of great Nonconformist evangelists. They were mainly Methodists, men like William Williams of Pantycelyn, Daniel Rowland and Howell Harris of Trefecca, and they became household names in nineteenth-century Wales.

The three spiritual leaders were all great preachers and evangelists but they were also writers of note. Thousands flocked to hear them preach and to sing their hymns, particularly the great flowing masterpieces of William Williams – his lyrics to Cwm Rhondda (Guide Me oh Thy Great Jehovah) still being sung in chapels and at rugby matches, over 200 years after his death.

Perhaps as much as anything it was the writings of the evangelists that were devoured in the towns and in the countryside. In their own way and in their own locations, William Williams, Daniel Rowland and Howell Harris were as notable and as influential as George Whitfield and John and Charles Wesley, and their sermons and written statements proved it.

What was remarkable in Welsh society during the late eighteenth century was the number of lower-class labourers and farm hands who were literate, able to read and write to a surprisingly high level. The man who deserved most of the credit for this and for what became the real roots of the Methodist Revival was the rector of Llanddowror, Griffith Jones.

In an age before formal education was offered to working-class men and women, Jones established a system of circulating schools that travelled the countryside – usually in the fallow times of the year – setting up house in barns, stables and anywhere they could find a welcome. In this way, Griffith Jones estimated that he had taught nearly 160,000 children to read, as well as perhaps 200,000 adults. When the population of Wales at that time was approximately 500,000, the significance of Jones's schools cannot be under estimated.[3]

Most of the people were taught to read Welsh, not English, and the medium used was the Bible. As a result, there was a huge interest in – and knowledge of – the scriptures but, in addition, spiritual growth and better education impelled Welshmen to begin thinking for themselves. They began to question the established order and not accept it simply because it had always been there.

The Methodist Revival and the Circulating Schools were inextricably linked and hugely pivotal in the growth of the nation: 'They changed the whole outlook of the working population, made them more enlightened, more receptive to new ideas, and more politically conscious.'[4]

The Directory failed to appreciate this, believing to the end that the Welsh were an oppressed, backward and poverty-stricken people. Perhaps they were, but the Welsh Dissenters were nowhere near as oppressed as, for example, the Roman Catholics in Ireland. The Welsh Dissenting groups were strong and they consoled each other by mutual faith and by their support for each other.

To an extent they were an oppressed minority group, but the spiritual awakening and political interest were greater forces than the Directory ever believed possible. And already, by the 1790s, the Industrial Revolution was beginning to make its mark on Wales. Better wages and better communication networks had begun to make a difference.

It was not something that happened overnight, but the appalling conditions in the mines, factories and steel works would not be tolerated for long by a people who had been made suddenly aware of their rights. Sooner or later there would be a reckoning – what the Directory failed to realise was that such a reckoning would be in their own time and on their own terms.

As much as the Methodist Revival and the Circulating Schools, the great iron works at Cyfarthfa and Dowlais were to change for ever the pattern of Welsh life. The infrastructure needed to run such industrial complexes – in particular improved wages, at least compared to those received by people still working in the rural economy – also brought improvements for the working people.

One other advantage of Wales, as far as the Directory was concerned, was that like Ireland it was distant from central government. While improved roads and the new canals created during the second half of the century had meant better means of communication, it still took several days – with coaches travelling at barely four or five miles an hour – for news from Wales to reach London.

Whether they were right or wrong, the above factors all influenced the Directory in its opinion of Wales and the Welsh. Perhaps one of their biggest mistakes, however, came in their misjudgement of the calibre and nature of the people. The Welsh radicals were certainly not made from the same stern mould as Wolfe Tone, Lord Fitzgerald and Arthur O'Connor. At best their arguments were academic exercises and none of them possessed the charisma of Tom Paine or the flamboyant Tone.

After the disaster of the Terror, Welsh radicalism floundered – and it did it in double quick time. After incurring the wrath of Pitt and his government, John Jones spent a number of years hiding in his native Wales. During this time, influenced by what was going on in France and by conversations with his fellow Welshmen, his political views gradually assumed a more conservative and decidedly mellower tone.

Richard Price had died in 1791, before the worst of the excesses, but he was in any case never a rabid revolutionary. He believed in the British constitution and praised the French national Assembly because it was, he felt, a truly representative body. He would have been mortified by the excesses of the Terror.

David Williams turned his back on French affairs, interpreting the increasing violence as a personal sleight. Even the infamous Iolo Morganwg took a step backwards and turned his hand to composing marching songs for the Glamorgan Volunteers – so much then for the most renowned and celebrated of all Welsh radicals.

One significant mistake made by the Directory was their belief that the Welsh Dissenters were as ready for release from their penury as the Catholics in Ireland. If that had indeed been the case, the Nonconformists would have been an easy target group for any invading force.

Unfortunately, what the French did not see was that the Dissenters in Wales were consoled by their faith, not revolutionised by it. The principal Dissenting sect at this time was the Methodists, and their belief in such theological issues as predestination gave them a sense of purpose that was able to with stand the hardest of blows.

Above all, the Acts of Union of 1536 had effectively smashed away the concept of nationalism within Wales. For over 200 years, ambitious Welshmen had, effectively, to become Englishmen in order to achieve. Working men and women were farmers or fishermen, tillers or weavers. The fact that they were Welsh farmers, fishermen, tillers and weavers hardly came into it. The Welsh language might be common, but being a Welshman was not.

In the minds of many, particularly for those across Offa's Dyke, Wales was just an extension of England – and a particularly troublesome extension it was, of no real value, the weather always bad and the people largely unresponsive. Even within Wales there was no groundswell of nationalism, no equivalent of the United Irishmen to fight for liberty.

If anything, there was a strong anti-revolutionary lobby among the ordinary men and women of Wales. Tom Paine was hanged in effigy in Cardiff and in several other towns, while public opinion was harnessed by the government which, in 1795, had suspended the Act of Habeas Corpus. This enabled officials to imprison or detain individuals without the benefit of trial. Revolutionaries and radicals found themselves hounded into a literal as well as a metaphorical corner. None of this permeated through to Hoche or the Directory.

It would take many, many years for serious nationalism to grow again in Wales – and perhaps that was the greatest mistake made by General Hoche and the Directory. They were effectively a 150 years too early.

Chapter 10

Went the Day Well?

Lord Milford, the Lord Lieutenant of Pembrokeshire, received news of the French landing at approximately 10.30 p.m. of the first day. Three despatches from Thomas Knox, outlining what had happened and what he was intending to do, were hurried to Picton Castle by a breathless messenger. There is no way of knowing for sure, but there would be a degree of symmetry if that messenger was the same one who had ridden hard all the way to summon Knox from Tregwynt earlier in the afternoon. It would be, at least, the romantic version.

Whoever the messenger was, Lord Milford's response to the news – which must have been frightening – was immediate. He wrote first to Lord Cawdor, a brief but explicit note that clearly outlined what the Lord Lieutenant of the county needed his fellow nobleman to do:

> To the Commanding Officer of the Loyal Pembroke Yeomanry Cavalry –
>
> These are to direct you on Receipt hereof or as soon as may be to march the men under your command to Haverfordwest. Dated at the Castle, Haverfordwest, this twenty second day of February 1797 – Milford.[1]

Milford next alerted and summoned the Cardigan Militia, then on guard at Golden Prison in Pembroke. He also wrote to Major James Ackland ordering him to assemble and march his Pembroke Volunteers directly to Haverfordwest. Lord Milford himself then travelled the four or five miles into Haverfordwest which had become the hub of the defending forces.

The first rumours of a French landing had begun circulating in Haverfordwest at around 6 p.m. that evening. The principal citizens quickly gathered together at the Castle Inn in the centre of the town in order to discuss their actions. As ever in Wales and Welsh affairs, they decided that their best course of action was to form a committee.

Captain Stephen Longcroft, the Navy Regulating Officer for Haverfordwest, agreed to lend his considerable weight and political clout to the committee. As the senior naval officer west of Swansea he had immense authority in the region and he immediately sent a runner to summon any sailors who might be available, perhaps waiting for ships or cargo, at Hubberston and Milford.

In 1797 Milford Haven was simply a safe anchorage, a natural fiord where ships could take on fresh water and wait safely for a favourable wind. The new town of Milford was barely a decade old and the subsequent Admiralty dockyard in the settlement still lay some five years in the future. It was not until 1814 that an even larger shipbuilding establishment – which became known as Pembroke Dockyard – was created up river at Pater Church Point.[2]

In the nineteenth century Pembroke Dock and, to some extent, Milford became the only truly industrial towns in the whole county of Pembrokeshire. That was in the future, however, and in 1797 the area was still a rural paradise. Despite its clear military attractions and benefits the Haven was a quiet backwater where little of note ever happened – at least not until February 1797.

The sailors on the waterway immediately complied with Longcroft's orders. From the crews of various small vessels then lying in the Haven, from the prize crew of a captured Dutch merchantman and from the officers and men of the revenue cutters *Speedwell* and *Diligence,* a force of 150 sailors was gathered together and marched inland to Haverfordwest. These included Lieutenants Perkins and Mears from the brig *Hope*, Lieutenants Hollingbury and Gilchrest from the Dutch prize and Lieutenants Dobbin and Hopkins of the revenue cutters.[3]

Lieutenants Dobbin and Hopkins, renowned and eager members of the revenue service, also managed to put ashore the 9 pounder guns from their cutters and while six of these cannons were mounted in Haverfordwest, two went on to Fishguard with the relieving force.[4]

It was time to send news of the landing to the wider world. On the orders of Lord Milford a messenger by the name of John Upcoat took the news from Tenby to the English counties on the other side of the Bristol Channel. According to legend he rowed across the Channel but such a feat, given the darkness and the state of the tide, is unlikely. From the towns along the south coast of the Bristol Channel, riders were despatched to take the alarm to all and sundry.

News of the invasion was widely known in London by 25 February but there had been rumours circulating in government circles the night before. By then, of course, events in Pembrokeshire had virtually played themselves out but that was not something that the government or the populace of London either knew or appreciated.

As soon as the news broke in Haverfordwest on 22 February, Captain Longcroft had sent the lugger *Valiant* to Cork to pass on the information to Admiral Sir Robert Kingsmill. At such a distance, however, there was little that either Kingsmill or the British government could do – at least for the moment.

Colonel Colby of the Pembrokeshire Militia had been present at the meeting in the Castle Hotel where he promised to do whatever he could to help. Consequently, as soon as the meeting broke up, he set off for Fishguard to find out for himself the state of affairs. He was accompanied on his ride by the Honourable William Edwardes, the son and heir of Lord William Edwardes, First Baron Kensington and MP for Haverfordwest.

They made a strange pair; Colby a much respected and admired local figure, Edwardes already renowned, at the age of just 19, as 'a boorish drunk'. He would go on to become an unpopular MP for the town before being displaced by General Sir Thomas Picton.[4] Nevertheless, during the invasion there was no hint of inebriation and Edwardes behaved in an exemplary fashion.

The night was exceptionally dark, there being no wind and very few stars to see by. Colby and Edwardes rode rapidly through the countryside, stopping only at high hedges and deep ditches. Just after midnight they eventually arrived at Fishguard Fort and there they found Lieutenant Colonel Thomas Knox. He was almost alone, apart from a small guard of Fencibles. Briefly, Knox filled in Colby with what he knew. At this stage it was not much. The French were on the Pencaer Peninsula but their numbers were unknown.

As they were talking, the Newport Division of the Fishguard Fencibles marched into the fort. Like Colby they had made a hurried journey through the darkness but, unlike him, they were on foot. Bowen's men, tired and footsore, threw themselves down to find rest wherever they could.

Knox must have been relieved to see Major Bowen's troops and he told Colby that he still intended to attack the French at dawn. There was a proviso; he would only attack if his forces were not too inferior to the enemy.

Knox later claimed that Colby had advised him to retreat, if needed, rather than stay and be wiped out. But whatever he chose to do he must keep the committee in Haverfordwest informed of his decision and actions.

Colby and Edwardes left Fishguard just after 1 a.m. and arrived back in Haverfordwest as dawn was breaking. There they heard the news that the forces from the south of the county, summoned by Lord Milford, were close at hand and duly went out to greet them. They then returned to the town at the head of the tired but eager relief force.

Lord Cawdor, at Stackpole Court to the south of Pembroke, had received the summons from Lord Milford around midnight. He had, however, already been told about the French landing at Fishguard and later wrote to the Duke of Portland:

> I received a message from a private friend at Haverfordwest on the 22nd of February at eleven at night with an account of the enemy being at Fishguard. I was collecting the troops when it was confirmed by the letter from the Lord Lieutenant.[7]

Cawdor's troop of cavalry was already partly assembled, prior to the funeral of a colleague which was due to take place the following morning. It was, therefore, a relatively simple matter to change their duties from ceremonial marching to one of war.

As soon as the troop was assembled, Cawdor set off for Pembroke, some six or seven miles to the north. There he picked up the Cardigan Militia and Ackland's Volunteers and began the long march to Haverfordwest. Their route lay up Bush Hill, then down the ridge to Pembroke Ferry, which was the quickest and easiest way of crossing the Cleddau River. The only alternative way of dealing with the river – a broad expanse which cut the county in two – was a twenty-mile hike around its upper reaches. Speed, however, was of the essence and Cawdor called in extra boats and ferrymen to facilitate the crossing.

A twenty-four hour, round-the-clock service was maintained by the ferrymen for the next eleven days, long after the alarm had passed. It was not simply dedication to duty, although there was undoubtedly considerable extra traffic across the river. Perhaps above all it was an example of Pembrokeshire men taking full advantage of a difficult situation.

The total extra cost, in terms of wages, ale and ferry charges, came to £24 11s 2d. It was not an insubstantial sum of money in those days.[8] The ferrymen would have said that they earned it; local wits, never averse to using the odd expletive, said they were 'just taking the piss!'

Luckily the weather was fine, although the night remained very dark. The boatmen knew the river, however, and there were no mishaps in getting the soldiers and their horses across. The Cleddau River was only the first of Cawdor's problems. Once again, his words sum up the matter:

> As soon as the Troop of Yeomen, the Cardigan Militia and the Pembroke Volunteers commanded by Captain Ackland had passed Pembroke Ferry, I forwarded to Haverfordwest and found it necessary, after some conversation with Lord Milford to offer to take the whole upon myself.[9]

Cawdor's ride through the dark Pembrokeshire countryside must have been a dramatic affair. He had little idea of what was facing him at

Fishguard – indeed, the French could even have been in Haverfordwest; he just knew that he had to act. He also knew the man he was dealing with and was well aware that decisive action was required; that, he knew, would never come from Lord Milford.

Lord Cawdor had only recently been ennobled, elevated to the peerage as Baron Cawdor of Castlemartin in June 1796. He was still commonly referred to as Squire Campbell, his real name and sobriquet, and had been a popular representative of Cardigan in Parliament for several years before his elevation to the peerage.

Cawdor was a Scot by birth with several significant holdings north of the border, but had married the heir to the old Lort estates in South Pembrokeshire. By 1797, he was worth a considerable fortune, his Stackpole estates covering 16,000 acres of land, from the banks of the Cleddau to the southern coast of the county. These estates alone brought him an income of £15,000 a year. It was the largest estate income in South Wales.[10]

Cawdor was a model estate manager and agriculturalist, taking an interest in things like crop rotation and the development of new breeds of livestock. Unusually for the time, he also had great concerns for, and interest in, the livelihood of his tenant farmers. As a result he was genuinely liked and appreciated by all of those who came into contact with him, before, during and after the invasion.

When he arrived at Haverfordwest in the early hours of 23 February, Cawdor found Lord Milford in a state of indecision. The Lord Lieutenant had alerted all of the forces he could think of but had done nothing else. The activity that had taken place, such as Colby's ride to Fishguard or Longcroft's decision to pull sailors off the ships in Milford Haven, had been individual efforts and had happened in spite of, rather than because of, Lord Milford.

Lord Milford, was not physically or emotionally capable of leading a relief force to help Knox at Fishguard. He was suffering from gout – almost an occupational hazard for noblemen at this time – and was acutely aware of his inadequacies as a military leader. Richard Philipps, to give him his correct name, was another newly created nobleman but in his early fifties he was neither as fit nor as dynamic as Lord Cawdor.

Choosing to delegate command of the relief forces to Lord Cawdor was probably the wisest decision Lord Milford could have made. It was not without some confusion however. Almost as soon as he had given the command to Cawdor, Lord Milford had second thoughts and decided to nominate John Colby, undoubtedly the most experienced of all the potential commanders, to the position. It made some sort of sense as Colby was the only one of three possible contenders for the position of commander in chief who had actually seen military service.

Cawdor, by his own admission, was inexperienced in the art of war, although he was also a very determined, dynamic and capable young man. The other contender, yet another Lieutenant Colonel, was Thomas Knox. Always eager and self-opinionated, he was sure that he should be the man to take charge. Others were equally sure that he should not. Lord Milford remained confused and unsure about almost everything and so he decided to leave it up to Cawdor and Colby.

The two men promptly sat down and thrashed it out. In the end it was decided that despite Colby's experience and position in the Militia, command should rest with Lord Cawdor, but that Colby would assist him in any way possible. It was a magnanimous decision by Colby and, as it turned out, the correct one. Knox, still in Fishguard, was neither consulted nor considered for the position. Cawdor, having debated the issue with Colby, now demanded that Lord Milford put his appointment down in writing.

With the command situation resolved, Cawdor lost no time in organising his forces. There appears to have been little or no resentment from Colby and the leader of the Pembrokeshire militia ably assisted his new commander. In a later commendation John Colby was singled out for the care and concern he showed 'in the disposition of each Corps, of which the Force was composed'.[11]

Joseph Adams, a friend and near neighbour of Cawdor, living at Holyland House outside Pembroke, was appointed principal aide de camp. Four others – the Hon. Captain Edwardes, Owen Phillips, Captain Davies of Coombe and John Phillips – were also appointed as aides de camp while Colby was officially nominated second in command.

In a desperate attempt to raise more men, an urgent request was sent to John Vaughan, Lord Lieutenant of Carmarthenshire. It went under Lord Milford's name but the urgency of the message and the precise wording indicate that it was quite probably dictated by Cawdor:

> Large body of French amounting to twelve hundred are landed at Fishguard. All the troops we have are gone direct there but I feel are inferior in numbers. If you can muster any armed men immediately they will be very serviceable. I am in great haste. Yours etc Milford, Haverfordwest Feb 23rd 1797.[12]

By 11 a.m. of Thursday 23 February the relieving force was assembled, en masse, in front of the Castle Inn. They were given bread, cheese and beer and at noon they marched out of Haverfordwest along the road to Fishguard.

It was not the most impressive military force the county had ever seen but they were all keen and willing enough to do battle in order to defend their country. It was a small gathering. A return now preserved at the Carmarthen Record Office shows that the total force, once they combined with the Fishguard Fencibles, was still woefully short of Tate's Legion which outnumbered them by at least two to one.

Cawdor's force was made up of 191 members of the Fishguard Fencibles, 150 sailors, 100 Cardigan Militia, ninety-three Pembroke Volunteers, forty-three Yeomanry Cavalry and a number of supernumeraries such as aides de camp and Thomas Nesbitt. In total it comprised twenty-two officers and 577 NCOs and men.[13]

This hotchpotch gathering of men – it would be misleading to call it an army – slowly made its way towards Fishguard. Their uniforms were diverse and their bands were undoubtedly playing different tunes and airs as they marched. They were armed with muskets, pistols and sabres and their two 9 pounder cannons were trundled along behind them in a pair of farm carts.

To the locals who flocked to the roadside to see them pass they must have seemed an incongruous sight. Yet they cheered them on their way and the young girls tossed them offerings of bread and cheese or some of the early daffodils that were beginning to appear under the hedgerows. They felt important, these farmers and sailors and, now, part-time soldiers. They knew that the safety of the whole country depended on them. They just didn't know how much.

Earlier that morning, Lieutenant Colonel Thomas Knox had made a fateful decision. Some French soldiers had been captured by Nesbitt's scouts during the night, one of them being an Irish deserter. According to some sources it was from this deserter that Knox learned that the strength of his enemy was somewhere in the region of fourteen hundred men.[14]

At first Knox was sceptical but every hour now brought fresh reports from Thomas Nesbitt. The figure was undoubtedly accurate. At first light Nesbitt arrived at the fort with the news that he had seen an advance guard of close to 800 men grouped around camp fires, some way inland from Careg Wastad Point. Knox himself now rode out to Pencaer in order to verify Nesbitt's report but was unable to get close enough to gain any more information.

It is difficult to see what Knox hoped to gain from this rather forlorn incursion into enemy territory. Nesbitt had spent the entire night on the Peninsula and was far better placed to give an accurate assessment of numbers than Knox could ever be. Possibly it shows a mistrust of this half-pay officer whom he really did not know – it is more likely that his ride displayed his indecision at the most critical time of his life.

Back in the fort, Knox considered his position; his own forces were pitifully few and there was no way that his 200 part-time soldiers could ever attack the French Legion. For all Knox knew the enemy might be the elite of the French army, and so he came to his decision.

He decided to retreat. The gunners in the fort were ordered to spike their cannons and dispose of their ammunition by tipping it over the cliff. Having issued these commands, Knox and the Fencibles marched out of the fort and headed towards Haverfordwest.

The artillery men, left behind once Knox had gone, had no intention of ruining their beloved guns. The weapons were, in any case, useless against anything other than a sea-borne assault and there was no way the French could ever take them and turn them against the town or a relieving army. The ammunition, limited as it was, they simply stacked into a hand cart and Ensign Bowen and his detachment took it away with them when they, the forlorn hope, brought up the rear.

For his decision to retreat on the morning of 23 February, young Knox was later castigated and accused of cowardice. Yet it is difficult to know what else he could have done, given the circumstances and his belief that he was facing an infinitely superior force. Purely in terms of numbers, he was opposed by an enemy that outnumbered him seven to one.

He firmly believed that his superiors wanted him to retreat, sticking to his point that Colonel Colby had advised him to do exactly that when he had come to the fort in the long reaches of the night. Colby later denied ever having given such advice but it is hard to believe that Knox would have conjured the statement out of thin air.

Knox had not long left Fishguard behind him when he met a messenger from Haverfordwest. It was a man by the name of William Fortune, carrying a message from the committee. Fortune was later to make a statement in defence of Knox, stating that he had been ordered to ride to Fishguard and pass on a crucial order:

> He was to go to Fishguard and inform you that they [the Committee] thought it most advisable for you to retreat towards Haverfordwest: and that a party of foot soldiers was expected at Haverfordwest 12 o'clock: and in the course of the evening Lord Cawdor with his cavalry: the both of which were to march on and join you.[15]

Fortune had left with his message before Colby returned from his scouting mission and while Cawdor's troop was still mustering. Had the committee realised that Cawdor would be in Haverfordwest so early it is doubtful that they would have suggested retreat. Taking up a position opposite Goodwick Beach, from where they could harass the French and hold a position that could be reinforced by Cawdor and Colby might have been an altogether better option.

Whatever his reasons, whatever drove him, Knox chose to retreat. The honourable way, the courageous way, would have been to stay and fight. Knox chose not to.

By midday he and his Fencibles had reached Trefgarne on the Haverfordwest road. There Knox called a halt and his soldiers settled down with their bread and cheese. At half past one the relieving force under Lord Cawdor arrived to join him and the British forces were united at last.

Significantly, however, behind them on the north coast of Pembrokeshire, the town of Fishguard lay open and undefended.

Chapter 11

A Time of Duty and Disaster

At Trefgarne in the early afternoon of 23 February there was a bitter and prolonged argument between Cawdor, Colby and Knox, the three major players on the British side. The cause of the discussion was simple – who was to take charge of the relief force?

Despite having delegated command to Lord Cawdor – and having put the decision down in writing – the indecisive Lord Lieutenant of the county now proceeded to change his mind again. It was typical of the ineptitude, indecision and confused thinking of Lord Milford at this time.

Almost as soon as the two forces united just after midday, a panting and sweating horseman, sent hotfoot from Lord Milford at Picton Castle, swept into the British camp with an urgent despatch. The message was worrying. Now Milford was saying that, despite his earlier decision, things would have to change. As Colonel Colby had held his commission far longer than the other two leaders, he was the man who should take charge of operations.

Whether Lord Milford felt that Cawdor had browbeaten him into his original decision is not known. Cawdor certainly could be direct and unwavering in his opinions but hardly overbearing. His own account is straightforward – he felt it expedient to offer to take command because Lord Milford was dithering. Urgency, Cawdor knew, was of paramount importance.

It is easy to imagine the scene at Trefgarne; the horseman preening himself, conscious of the importance of his message; the officers tentatively handling the despatch, wondering who it should go to; everyone desperate to know what it was all about.

The letter declaring Lord Milford's change of heart was brought first to Lieutenant Colonel Thomas Knox. At that time Cawdor just happened to have ridden out ahead of the force, scouting the area around Pencaer. As second in command Colby was busy seeing to the disposition of the troops. Knox was the only one of the senior staff the messenger and the junior officers who first received him could find.

The message confused Knox. For some strange reason he had not even considered Cawdor to be in command, believing that the position was his and his alone. Despite his recent retreat he was the only one of the senior officers to have actually faced the French. He knew the lie of the land and arrogantly believed that his rank and position entitled him to command.

He was still studying the letter when, soon afterwards, Cawdor returned from his reconnaissance. He was immediately confronted by an angry Thomas Knox who thrust the message under his nose.

'What the devil is this?' he demanded. 'I am in command here.'

Cawdor stared him down. He then passed the note to Colby. For a moment or two there was silence, before Colby, astutely realising that this was neither the time nor the place to debate the issue of seniority, told them both that they should ignore Lord Milford's latest epistle. The Lord Lieutenant of the county was not here with the army, he said, and should therefore have no say in the running of the campaign.

'I, for one,' Colby declared, bowing to Cawdor, 'am happy to waive my rights to command, no matter what Lord Milford might say. I will continue to serve, my Lord, as your right hand man.'

He turned to Thomas Knox. 'I advise you, sir, to do the same.'

Knox was unhappy, however. His feelings had been hurt and his temper, always short at the best of times, was perilously close to boiling over. Cawdor could see the resentment in the man but there was more at stake than soothing the ruffled feathers of someone he considered a dilettante. Colby had given him his lead.

'This is no time for discussions about military etiquette,' Cawdor snapped at Knox. 'I require only your assurance that you will place your men under my control. Otherwise you may quit the field.'

Knox fretted and fumed. He strode away, hesitated and then returned in a classic display of petulance. But eventually – and with a great deal of reluctance – he agreed. Lord Cawdor would take command and there, for the time being at least, the matter rested.

At about 2.30 p.m. the combined British relief force finally left the shelter of Trefgarne Rocks and proceeded along the road towards Fishguard. The mood in the ranks was more sober now. The men from the south of the county, the sailors and the Yeomanry Cavalry had spoken to the Fishguard Fencibles who had seen the French at first hand and, perhaps for the first time, began to have an idea of what they were up against.

It was a time for solemn thoughts and introspection – for silent prayers for some of them. But nobody even considered running away, or turning tail and heading back to Haverfordwest. They were, all of them, set on their course and so they ploughed steadily onwards. As dusk fell the British forces were just one mile from the centre of Fishguard.

* * *

For Tate and the Legion Noire the day had not gone well. It was disappointing as things had begun with such optimism and a fair, if limited, degree of success. Matters had gone downhill from there.

Colonel Tate knew that he had to find supplies for his men. Equally as important, he had to obtain transport to help him with the march northwards. In particular he needed carts and horses to carry the sick and the supplies and to pull the ammunition. Carts of any description, from hay wagons to country carriages, would be essential to hold the huge quantities of food that he was contemplating gathering from the houses of the locals. There was no way he could break out towards Chester and Liverpool until this transport had been found.

Speed was of the essence. It meant that while the best troops in the Legion, the grenadiers in particular, were acting as the advance guard and holding positions like Carnwndda and Carn Gelli, gathering supplies became the job of the convict soldiers. As daylight strengthened and a weak, watery sun began to appear over the eastern horizon, parties of them were pulled together and sent out on foraging missions.

It was Tate's biggest mistake. While the recalcitrant chasseurs were corralled together on the headland of Careg Wastad Point they were able to cause no major problems. It was a relatively small and confined area where they were easily martialled or ordered around. Any discipline problems that might occur could be dealt with as they arose. Once they were despatched across the Peninsula on their sorties to find food and wagons, however, the soldiers were beyond Tate's reach and out of his control. For men who had been virtually prisoners in the gaols of Brest and on Castagnier's ships the sudden sense of freedom went as quickly to their heads as the alcohol they now found and devoured:

> Eight hundred convicts were dispatched [*sic*] on marauding expeditions, in small parties, about four miles along the coast, and nearly the same distance inland; they found a quantity of port wine in every house; the wine had been picked up along the coast a few days previous. Intoxication and disorder were the natural consequences.[1]

The figure of 'eight hundred' is probably a gross exaggeration but the rest of the story is true enough. A Portuguese coaster, carrying many cases of good quality port and wine, had been wrecked on the coast of north Pembrokeshire only a month or so before and virtually every house in the region was well stocked with the remnants of the ship's looted cargo.

Wrecking was, and still remains, a romantic myth best left to historical novelists. The Pembrokeshire people were not wreckers but they were not averse to a little judicious looting. If a ship was cast ashore, her cargo washed onto the beaches and cliffs, it was fair game. Hence the houses full of recently acquired wine.

Smuggling was rife in the region, as it was in all coastal areas where people tried desperately to beat the tax and import duties set by the government. This was particularly the case in Northern Pembrokeshire where the relatively close proximity of the Isle of Man – still, then, an independent kingdom, free from tax and, as a consequence, a smuggler's paradise – made trade in illicit goods an attractive option for all sorts of people. It meant that the houses of the Peninsula would ordinarily have been full of illegal spirits, tobacco and other luxury goods. As the poet Rudyard Kipling once declared:-

> Five and twenty ponies
>
> Trotting through the dark –
>
> Brandy for the parson
>
> 'Baccy for the clerk,
>
> Laces for a lady, letters for a spy
>
> And watch the wall my darling, while the gentlemen go by.[2]

That would have been a fairly accurate picture of Pembrokeshire in the late eighteenth century with everyone from the local vicar to the landed gentry being involved in some way, major or minor, with smuggling enterprises. Add in the Portuguese coaster with its cargo of looted wine and it all spelled disaster for Tate and his band of warriors.

What quickly transpired was that the men of the Legion Noire decided to relieve the farmers and local gentry of their ill-gotten gains. Within the space of a few short hours the convict marauders were either hopelessly drunk or painfully, excruciatingly ill, as anything that was drinkable, edible, or in any way consumable was happily guzzled down.

Chickens in the farmhouse gardens stood no chance. Wine and brandy disappeared at a rate of knots as the eager convict soldiers cut a swathe across the land. And as the proceedings on Pencaer descended into a drunken melee, skirmishes and incidents took place between the invaders and the local populace, most of them members of the so-called 'lower classes'. Several of the incidents are worthy of mention.

* * *

People in nearby St David's heard news of the landing early in the day. The cathedral and small town were hidden from the sea, having been being built in a hollow as a precaution against marauding Norsemen back in the eighth and ninth centuries. It didn't work; the church and its surrounding community were burned on several occasions.

While the French sailors and soldiers of the Legion Noire failed to spot the town, the Welsh were luckier – or perhaps more used to surveying the sea. From the hills, the beaches and the foreshore, the inhabitants of St David's quickly noticed Castagnier's four ships and, more importantly, knew them for what they were.

A group of locals went immediately to the cathedral and began to strip the protective lead sheeting from its roof. These sheets were then handed to the town blacksmith to be made into bullets. It was not something that was done lightly and there was a heated debate between townspeople and the Dean and cathedral authorities who were, quite understandably, concerned about losing the protective lead sheeting from their roof.

In the end pragmatism triumphed. Along with the limited amount of gunpowder held in the town, the bullets were made and duly handed out to the citizens. The following day dozens of people began flocking to join Lord Cawdor's troops or, in many instances, simply headed off towards Fishguard under their own steam.

Many years later, when alterations and improvements were being undertaken at a local farmhouse, a bag of bullets made from St David's Cathedral lead, was found hidden in one of the walls. They had been placed there along with a scribbled note stating that they had been cast in the year of the invasion and were intended for use if the French should come again.[3]

Resident in St David's at that time was the engineer Henry Whiteside, an Englishman who had been born and raised in Liverpool. Originally a designer and maker of musical instruments, he had decided to change career and was in the area to help rebuild the Smalls lighthouse. Situated out in the approaches to St George's Channel, twenty miles west of Marloes, the light on the top of the deadly Smalls Rock was vital in warning shipping of dangerous rocks and shoals.

If that sounds strange – a musical-toy maker building a lighthouse – it must be remembered that at the end of the eighteenth century there was no such thing as uniformity, either in the design of the warning lights or in the training and qualifications of the men who made them: 'There was, as yet, no such thing as an archetypal engineer, let alone a civil or marine specialist. The qualifications and bureaucracy of the modern profession did not exist.'[4]

Whiteside may not have been an engineer of the same class as Robert Louis Stevenson's forefathers, but he was skilled in his trade and commanded the respect of the men who worked for him. He knew the dangers of the western oceans and was brave and honest in his attempts to defeat them.

Now, however, Whiteside had other dangers in mind. As soon as he learned of the French landing he sent out a message to men at nearby Solva, many of them seamen who had been helping him build the Smalls lighthouse. They rushed to St David's, where Whiteside armed them with sporting guns and marched them off towards Fishguard.

At Carngerwil Farm below Carn Gelli they ran into a party of five Frenchmen. Almost immediately both sides opened fire. It has never been clear who fired first but when the smoke from the black powder muskets drifted away, one French soldier was dead and another two seriously wounded. One of the Solva sailors had also been wounded. The Frenchmen decided they had had enough and took to their heels, leaving Whiteside and his men to cheer their success and gather in the wounded.

It just so happened that Colonel Tate witnessed the encounter. He was on the top of Carn Gelli at the time, surveying the surrounding countryside. He supposedly made the comment – although the source is not always felt to be totally accurate – that if raw, untrained men could form up and conduct themselves in such a cool and collected manner, then the future did not look too bright for his poor soldiers. What would happen, he asked himself, when they came up against the might of the British Army?[5]

The dead French soldier was later buried in the field where he was shot. The area is still known locally as Parc-y-Francwr (Frenchman's

Park or Frenchman's Field) a tribute that the French convict soldier could never have hoped to claim in his life.

It was not all one-way traffic, however. That morning, up on the Pencaer Peninsula, two Welsh farm labourers attacked a party of French soldiers they found trying to drive away their livestock. In the ensuing scuffle, the two Pembrokeshire men were killed along with one of the invaders. The two farmers were the first Welsh fatalities of the campaign.

Again on Pencaer, a convict soldier hammered on the door of one cottage and demanded food from the householder. While he was eating, the man of the house crept up behind him and smashed him over the head with a chair leg. Knocked senseless, the Frenchman became an easy prisoner.

Several of the stories told about the events of 23 February are difficult to authenticate. They were told orally and passed on from generation to generation, thus becoming part of folklore. However, given the chaos and confusion of that difficult and dangerous day, they – and other events like them – probably did have their basis in truth.

One example of this factual and mythological coming-together is the often-told story of an old man who decided to fraternise with the invaders in an attempt to protect his house and the eighty guineas he had secreted in the building. The old man, apparently, provided the French foragers with food and drink and then joined them in their rowdy celebrations. His tongue loosed by the wine, the man soon disclosed his secret stash and found himself eighty guineas poorer. If the story is not true then it certainly should be!

One of the better-known legends of the invasion concerns the ticking clock at Brestgarn Farm House. Home of the Reverend David Bowen, Brestgarn still sits high on the Pencaer Peninsula and in 1797 it was an obvious target for the French looters.

According to the story, a drunken French soldier stumbled into the house looking for more drink. He heard a click from behind him and in his fuddled and stupefied state thought it was the sound of a pistol being cocked. He turned and fired – straight through the face of a grandfather clock which stood in the hallway of the house.

The clock is still held at Brestgarn, although sadly it is not on show. It remains in situ, however, complete with bullet-hole. But whether the hole was put there by a drunken French soldier or carefully added by a hot poker in the days after the invasion remains a matter of conjecture.

Another equally ludicrous incident took place not far away from Brestgarn when a drunken Frenchman was hauling up the bucket at a well in order to relieve his thirst. Someone stole up behind him and tipped him unceremoniously down the well shaft. Surprisingly, he lived to tell the tale, so that one we know to be true.

The undoubted hero of the hour was Jemima Nicholas. In some accounts of the invasion she is called the town cobbler, in others a part-time shoe mender and in some, the wife of the town cobbler. Any of the descriptions is possible. She was also referred to as Jemima Fawr, Great Jemima.

In all probability the epithet does not refer to her size, as many historians and writers have reported, but to the immensity of the deeds ascribed to her during the invasion scare. She might well have been physically large – she would have to have been robust and strong enough to carry out the job of town cobbler – but the Amazon-type figure of popular legend who could beat any man in a fist fight is little more than a myth.

As if to confirm this, when Jemima died in 1832 a note was added to the parish register by the vicar of the town stating that she was known as Jemima Fawr because of her great deeds during the French landing of 1797.[6] There was no reference to her size. However, local legend was already declaring that she could take on any man at wrestling or fisticuffs, a classic case of the old adage 'When the legend gets bigger than the truth, print the legend.'[7]

What is certainly known about Jemima is that she marched out onto the Pencaer Peninsula and, single-handedly, captured a number of French soldiers. In some accounts the number is given as six, in others it is twelve. She then supposedly went back to look for more but by then the French could see her coming and they promptly fled back to camp.

In all probability the twelve captives – if it was twelve – were already cowed, cold and very drunk. Even so, that should not stop anyone admiring Jemima's deed. There has been, of late, a great deal of debate about Jemima, some writers even doubting that she ever existed. Whether she was actually awarded a pension by the grateful government is another point of debate. Some writers believe that a handsome award of £50 per annum was given to her every year until her death in 1832. Others believe she received nothing.

Pension or no pension, the town and people of Fishguard were strong in their admiration of Jemima Fawr. A tombstone in St Mary's Church in the centre of the town – erected by public subscription to mark the centenary of the invasion – declared that this was a memorial 'In Memory of Jemima Nicholas of this town, the Welsh heroine who boldly marched out to meet the French invaders.'

There is no mention of Jemima Fawr here, you will notice. Not surprisingly, she has now become the 'Welsh heroine'.

It is impossible to know how many local inhabitants fell foul of the French marauders on this day. Not everyone who came into contact with the invaders was killed. One woman, by the name of Mary Williams – wife of the man who fled to the fort during the first night of the invasion, claiming to have been captured and wounded – was detained close to her home at Caerlem and shot in the leg by a party of Frenchmen. She was then raped. Whether or not Williams and his wife were cashing in on the fear of the time is not known but there seems to have been no reason to doubt Mary's statement. Again, local legend states that she was awarded a pension but it has proved impossible to verify this.

The number of French casualties sustained on 23 February is also somewhat unclear. A return prepared by Lieutenant Colonel Knox indicated that the bodies of two Frenchmen had been found near Tregwynt. The local people admitted to killing two more. Another account gives a total of three Frenchmen killed, a further two later dying of their wounds.[8]

Such was the chaos and confusion on Pencaer that even the French had little or no real understanding of their casualties. Stories quickly became lurid and the tale of convict soldiers cutting the throat of one of their number, for reasons that have never been made clear – and then throwing his body over the cliff into the sea – cannot be proved, one way or another.

What is known is that the damage caused by the Legion Noire – the marauding convicts and the more controlled grenadiers – was vast. In the aftermath of the invasion over £1,000 was paid out in compensation to people who had lost livestock and possessions.[9]

John Mortimer of Trehowel found that when he returned home after the French surrender the damage to his house was astronomical. Nearly all of the window frames had been removed to be used as fuel for camp fires and a valuable clock had simply vanished. Someone told him that it had been spirited out of the house onto one of the French ships. It was never seen again.

Many of Mortimer's mattresses had been cut up to make trousers for the soldiers – a new slant on the phrase sans culottes! The feather stuffing from the mattresses was spread throughout the house and the dining room table branded by hot pokers used to warm the mulled wine that the French officers had made. Every single one of his chickens and pigs had been eaten.

Tate's offer of his sword as compensation cannot have been particularly satisfactory for John Mortimer. The government's later compensation, to the tune of £130, must have made the inconvenience and the damage rather easier to bear.[10]

* * *

Tate did not realise it, but fate had almost presented him with an unexpected and certainly unlooked-for chance of victory early on the evening of 23 February. All day Cawdor and his relieving force had been inching closer and closer to Fishguard. During their march Cawdor had made a point of speaking to the people they encountered, dozens of them, perhaps hundreds, who were fleeing from Fishguard.

There seemed to be a very real threat of panic overwhelming the region and so Cawdor set about alleviating the problem in the best way he knew. He deliberately spread a rumour, informing everyone that: 'A force superior to that of the enemy was advancing and urged them to arm themselves in the best manner they could and join it.'[11]

Certainly many gentlemen and yeomen chose to stop running and take his advice. Soon his army was augmented by hundreds of men of all classes, some armed with sporting guns, others with scythes and bill hooks. Most were on foot but some had horses. Regardless of how they travelled, by the end of the day Cawdor's little army numbered well over a thousand.[12] About 650 of them were part-time soldiers and sailors from the ships at Milford, the rest willing but totally untrained volunteers.

At the farmhouse of Manorowen, at approximately 5 p.m., came the first contact between the relieving force and the French. Manorowen lay at the foot of the Pencaer peninsula, within easy striking distance for the more adventurous of the foraging convicts. It was also fresh ground for men who had, by now, cleaned out most of the houses on the Peninsula.

As Cawdor's army advanced, a small party of French foragers was spotted in the grounds, seeming to be making for the summer house. Cawdor quickly despatched a troop of his Yeomanry cavalry to intercept them.

Whooping with delight the riders swept towards the Frenchmen. Shots were exchanged but it was by now already dark and the French were able to slip away in the gloom. Nobody seemed to be hurt and now, drawing up his troops along the roadway, Cawdor and his staff went into a hurried conference.[13]

Cawdor knew that reinforcements, in the shape of regular troops, would eventually arrive and until then his task was one of containment. Anxious to prevent the French breaking out from their positions on the Pencaer Peninsula, Cawdor and Colby decided on drastic action. Despite the darkness and with only limited intelligence on the French dispositions, they decided to launch an immediate attack.

Battlefield intelligence, or an understanding of the terrain over which you must fight, has always been a crucial element in any military action. Yet Cawdor, despite having ridden forward to reconnoitre the area, had no real awareness of the land over which he was proposing to advance. This was where Knox should have advised him, but for some reason he said nothing. Possibly the young man was still sulking, possibly he was as ignorant of the terrain as Cawdor.

In hindsight the decision to attack was a foolish choice, one that could have backfired and brought total disaster. The night was pitch black and the only access onto the Peninsula was by means of long, narrow lanes, ideal for small groups of foragers but no use at all for an advancing army.

At best the British front would be only three or four men abreast; the rest would be packed together in the rear, unable to fire or charge and certainly unable to deploy across the fields. If the French fire was accurate the relieving soldiers, sailors and civilians would be sitting targets for the enemy.

Cawdor was driven by the clear instinct that he needed to pin down the enemy. Colby and the others agreed with him – although someone with Colby's experience should have known better – and so the troops were deployed and the message to advance was given. It was probably the one British mistake in the whole campaign and in the end Cawdor missed disaster by a hair's breadth.

Now, in hindsight, it is hard to see what Cawdor and Colby thought they could achieve by such a risky manoeuvre. It was a gamble as Colby, more than anyone else, fully understood. But it was a gamble worth taking, he and Cawdor decided. What they had seen and heard of the French thus far did not fill them with trepidation or dread – perhaps one small push was all that was needed to dislodge the invaders and send them scurrying back to France.

Dragging their cannon behind them, the British advanced steadily onto the Peninsula. It was a march of confusion, soldiers treading on the heels of the men in front of them, civilian volunteers tripping over their pitchforks and shovels. The noise of their coming, the shouts and curses of the men alone, would have disturbed the dead.

At Trefwrgy, a bare half mile from the French advance guard, Cawdor suddenly halted them. In a solid, heaving mass the men climbed out of the lane and tried their best to deploy on a broader front. It was difficult because of the darkness and the inexperience of the men involved, but it was better than the chaos of trying to walk together down the lane.

As Cawdor's men were milling about in the darkness, Barry St Leger and his grenadiers out in front of the men on Carnwndda could hear the beat of the enemy drums, the whistling of their fifes and the clashing of their accoutrements. It was still too dark to see the enemy soldiers but St Leger knew that fate had given him a chance.

'Down,' he hissed at his men, 'everybody lies flat to the earth.'

He watched as the 200 grenadiers flattened themselves into the gorse and heather, their black uniforms making them almost invisible in the gloom.

'Nobody fires until I give the word,' he whispered and then lay back to wait.

Lying there in the darkness, St Leger knew only too well the precariousness of his position. He had no idea who he was facing, either the quality or quantity of the enemy troops. For all he knew they could be the cream of the British Army and, despite his inexperience, he was knowledgeable enough to realise that he would have to operate as if the men he was facing were troops from the elite Coldstream Guards.

St Leger also understood that once the grenadiers opened fire the British would take the first volley and then regroup. That was the danger point, the time when he and his men could be quickly overrun unless their first volley was devastating. Everything depended on the element of surprise and that first shock encounter when volley fire, not individual sharp-shooting, offered the best chance of success.

His plan almost worked. At the last moment Cawdor decided to abandon the attack. Whether or not somebody had discovered St Leger's ambush – Thomas Nesbitt perhaps – or the frantic attempts to deploy in the darkness had convinced him of the foolishness of the action, he decided to halt the advance and pull back.

One account tells of a gentleman volunteer by the name of Mansell who was present during the advance. After stumbling up the deep lane for some time, he and his comrades were finally halted. The time was about 8.00 p.m. and the blackness, with no light pollution and few stars, was absolute. Word came down the line, he said, that they were to go no further: 'The ambush had been discovered. There were 200 of them lying flat on their bellies. They wished us to begin the action as by that means they could see us.'[14]

Whatever the reason, Cawdor had decided that to proceed further was both foolish and dangerous. He would wait for tomorrow. The troops fell back to Manorowen and from there to the town of Fishguard itself. It was not an easy withdrawal and seeing the confusion Cawdor must have realised that his decision to pull back was the correct one

Up on the Peninsula, Barry St Leger listened to the sound of the British withdrawal, the curses of the men and the clanging of metal against metal, with mixed feelings. He was not a trained soldier and had no particularly bloodthirsty feelings, but he was a serving officer in the Legion Noire and he had a duty to perform.

Had the British soldiers come under St Leger's guns he would undoubtedly have opened fire – with, probably, devastating results. But deep inside the young man, something rebelled at the thought of the death and destruction he would have unleashed.

He held his breath as the grenadier he had sent out to report on the British movements came panting back up the slope. The man threw himself down beside him.

'They've gone, sir,' he reported, 'pulled right back. Not a sign of them anywhere.'

St Leger nodded and rose to his feet. He would have to go and report to Colonel Tate, knowing that fate had given them a great chance of victory but, at the last moment, snatched it away again.

Chapter 12

The Fleet Leaves

L ong before Lord Cawdor almost brought his army to disaster, events in the French camp had been progressing – and not always satisfactorily. As the day wore on, Colonel Tate had become more and more depressed. Not only was the majority of the Legion Noire out of control, many of them were becoming openly mutinous.

Several incidents were reported to Tate of men turning their weapons on their officers, threatening to shoot them if they attempted to drag them or their comrades away from the warmth of the camp and picket fires. Discipline, always tenuous, seemed to have broken down.

It was a difficult and dangerous time in the operation and, strangely, it was at this moment that Commodore Castagnier decided he would weigh anchor and leave.

There had never been any intention of the French ships remaining off the Welsh coast. Their job had been to transport the men of the Legion Noire from France to Britain, nothing more. That job had been done. As far as the sailors were concerned, what happened ashore was none of their business, control and disposition of the troops being down to Tate and his officers.

It was never clear why Castagnier had lingered so long. The last of the soldiers had gone ashore early on the morning of that Thursday, 23 February, but the commodore and his ships had not, as might be expected, immediately pulled up anchors and set sail for home. For several hours they had sat off Careg Wastad Point, the four ships riding easily in the gentle swell and the officers and men seeming to enjoy the unseasonal warm sunshine on their backs.

The tiny fleet had no purpose, no reason to stay now that the Legion was ashore. There had never been any intention of re-embarking the troops – and the question has to be asked; why did Castagnier not clear out earlier in the day? That would have been the most sensible and safest way of behaving.

Indeed, the longer the French ships tarried, the more parlous their situation became. To be caught on the coast by British frigates would have spelled disaster. Trapped against the shore there would have been no room to manoeuvre and nowhere to run.

Castagnier knew that he had stayed far longer than he should have done. Quite apart from the false sense of security his presence created in the minds and hearts of the convict soldiers up on Pencaer there was a real danger in remaining so close, for so long, to the British coast. Castagnier was no fool and it did not take the most astute tactical or military brain to realise that, even now, the Royal Navy would be marshalling its forces against him.

He was right. Already, in response to the earlier sightings of the French squadron off Lundy, the frigates *Shannon*, *Beaulieu* and *Mercury* had been sent to the Severn Estuary. Admiral Alexander Hood, Lord Bridport as he was universally known, and his Channel Fleet were also preparing to sail. Over the Channel in Cork, Admiral Kingsmill had been made aware of the French presence and his ships were ready to sail at a moment's notice.

Ominously, the forces being put together against Castagnier's small fleet were overwhelming. And so, in the mid-afternoon of 23 February the commodore sent a messenger ashore, announcing that he was about to sail.

Informed of Castagnier's decision, Tate and several of his senior officers signalled the flagship for a boat and rowed out to the *Vengeance*. It is unlikely that Tate went with the intention of persuading Castagnier to stay. According to the Commodore it was just the opposite:

Thursday, February 23rd – At 2.00 a.m. all the troops had been landed with arms, provisions and ammunition. At 4.00 p.m. Colonel Tate and his officers informed me that they had no more need of my services. According to my instructions I caused a process-verbal to be drawn up in the presence of the staff of the squadron and prepared to carry out the rest of my instructions. At 5.10 p.m. the squadron was under sail.[1]

The process-verbal that Castagnier referred to in his log was a document signed by twenty-four officers, from the Legion and from the fleet. Among them were Tate, Castagnier himself and Colonel Le Brun, the Legion's second in command. The document confirmed that Castagnier had carried out his duty and that there was no longer any need for him to remain.

A complex series of codes and signals was arranged should Castagnier or others reappear at some stage in the future – a rather strange arrangement given that Tate was still intending to quit the area as soon as he could and march northwards.[2]

The signals included the ships flying a red flag and the simultaneous discharge of muskets and rockets. The rationale behind such arrangements can only have been to facilitate a follow up expedition to reinforce the bridgehead that had been established on British soil. Tate knew that Castagnier would carry a message to that effect and to that extent he was right. But if he had hoped that the Directory would respond immediately he was gravely mistaken.

The Directory had already lost interest in the Legion Noire and Tate must have realised that the French government was a lot happier to see him and his Legion depart than it ever would be to witness a return. General Hoche had already left Brest for the Low Countries and with him had gone all hope for what now seemed to be a doomed operation.

Tate was already disconsolate and despairing of his troops. He had seen their drunken behaviour and had even witnessed their defeat in the small skirmish below Carn Gelli. He can have had no illusions about the success of his landing and of the inevitable fate of his force should they attempt to break out.

Possibly – and it remains mere speculation – he had decided to remain on Pencaer and wait, if not for reinforcements then at least for an honourable surrender. Such a move would have been in keeping with his attitude and emotions at this time.

Whatever the reasons, just after 4.00 p.m., Tate was rowed ashore and Castagnier prepared to set sail. The Colonel climbed out of the long boat onto the rocks below Careg Wastad Point, watched it haul around and took his pistols, one in each hand. He fired them into the air and, presently, was answered by a return salute from the *Vengeance*.

Then the French ships pulled up their anchors, swung around and, with all sails set, headed off into the gathering gloom of evening. By 5.30 it was as if they had never been there.

Up on the heights of Pencaer the soldiers of the Legion Noire watched the ships sail away. Most of them had a bitter taste in their mouths. As long as Castagnier had remained there, just off the coast, there was always a chance of escape. Now, with the fleet gone, they stood unaided and afraid on the British mainland.[3]

* * *

There has always been a degree of confusion about Castagnier's departure, arising partly from the Commodore's delay in sailing and partly from the opinions of the French soldiers.

Many early writers or commentators believed that the soldiers had been deserted, abandoned to their fate, when the ships sailed away. It was a point of view with which most of the Legion would have agreed and such emotions may well have been passed on from the French prisoners themselves to eyewitnesses at the time:

> It was a madcap enterprise, and it leaves more than one riddle unsolved. There is much probability in the theory that the expedition was really despatched in order to get a number of convicts and poor soldiers lodged and fed at the expense of the British. No other theory accounts for the sudden departure of the French ships.[4]

From the start the soldiers of the Legion Noire had been badly informed about the intentions of the operation. There is no reason to suppose that Tate or any of the others had now chosen to enlighten them about their task and the details of the affair. That was not the way things were done in the French – and British – army at the time. Soldiers, even poor ones like the members of the Legion Noire, were expected simply to do their duty and not ask questions.

Tate's soldiers had little or no idea why the ships were there or not there, and it is easy to see how the feelings of abandonment took root as Castagnier's fleet sailed away. Most of them worked in the immediate, having little thought of tomorrow or of wider philosophical issues.

Even to those on the other side of the quarrel, the residents of Fishguard and the members of the relieving force, the sudden departure of the ships was a mystery: 'The French warships raised their anchors and sailed right across the Channel in the direction of the Irish coast. What induced the Commodore to do this is not known.'[5]

For the men of the Legion Noire it was not a mystery, it was abandonment and betrayal. As a consequence their depression and mood of sullen anger, already fuelled by wine and other alcohol, increased greatly. Unfortunately for Colonel Tate this anger was directed not at the enemy but at their own leaders.

It was not just in the rank and file that there were problems of morale. The Irish officers were appalled at the situation. It was not that they were angry or upset at finding themselves part of an invading army on British soil. They knew that was what the intention had been right from the start, but they were now part of an invading army that was on the point of disintegrating. The consequences of impending defeat and capture were suddenly brought close to home.

Barry St Leger sought out his two Irish colleagues, Morrison and Tyrell. They sat and discussed the situation and St Leger managed to gain their approval for a plan he had in mind. With the two men in tow his next port of call was Colonel Tate himself.

'We have had enough, Colonel,' he declared. 'We intend to quit the Legion.'

They would slip away, he said, and blend into the countryside. Tate's response was to ask St Leger to wait a while before taking off into the unknown. When St Leger questioned the wisdom of this, the Colonel was clear – he had decided to surrender.[6]

It was thunderous news for the Irish officers and, far from reassuring them, it had suddenly placed them in an even more difficult situation. They had no real desire to fight the British. The performance of the legion so far had convinced them that, if it came to combat, their chances of success were decidedly slim.

But if Tate was genuine in his decision to surrender, their future looked even more uncertain. The rank and file of the Legion were French and therefore engaged in an act of war. Come surrender they would be treated as prisoners of war. The Irish, on the other hand, were guilty of treason and treachery – and that might well mean the death penalty for all of them.

Robert Morrison in particular expressed concern about finding himself in Wales. Yet how much truth there is in his statement, taken after the surrender, remains doubtful. He knew when he was taken off the *Cassard* that his services were needed because he spoke English – therefore the Legion was intended for an English speaking country. As the *Cassard* and her compatriots were already bound for Ireland, that left only mainland Britain.[7]

Castagnier's departure was clearly something of a watershed, even though he and Tate had not intended it to be. Tate himself was now in a state of abject worry and concern. Above all, he was confused.

The whole of the country seemed to be up in arms against him – not something he had expected or been led to believe would happen. In fact, it was diametrically opposed to what he had been told would be the case. The French plan hinged on the belief – the mistaken belief as it turned out – that the Welsh would rise up to join his forces. When the opposite occurred it was heart-breaking.

With his troops out of control, drunk, ill or mutinous, Tate dithered and found himself torn a dozen different ways. He felt desperately sorry for the Irish in the Legion, officers and enlisted men alike, understanding their plight only too well. But, at the same time, he knew that a splendid chance to strike at the hated English was being wasted by his drunken troops.

Indecision and an inability to take the hard decision – qualities necessary in any commander – seemed to have dropped over Tate like a shroud. Where he should have been dynamic and vital he displayed only lethargy.

As Robert Morrison later stated, Tate's words in response to his declared intention to leave were simple: 'I don't know what to say.'[8] That brief statement summed up the indecision and the futility of the enterprise. It also summed up William Tate at this precise moment in time.

Meanwhile, the situation on the Peninsula had gone from bad to worse. Drunkenness, robbery and theft were widespread.

The church in the tiny village of Llanwnda was broken into and vandalised. The church Bible was ripped, the soldiers using the pages as fuel for their fires and for toilet paper. Valuable church records were destroyed and the communion plate was stolen.

Mutiny was common. Morrison later deposed that: 'The troops behaved very badly in robbing and plundering ... the officers sentenced one man to be shot for robbery but the soldiers would not shoot him.'[9]

Even allowing for the French belief and policy that soldiers should 'live off the land', finding their provisions from enemy territory, the depredations carried out that Thursday seem to be well past normal. In many instances things had gone beyond pillaging and foraging – now it was a case of downright robbery.

Everywhere Tate looked there seemed to be only disaster and disorder and nothing he could do would stop the pillaging. As he later told several incredulous locals: 'He had often been in battle, over his shoes in blood; but he had never felt such a sensation as when he put his foot on British ground – that his heart failed him, in a way he could not describe.'[10]

He tried hard to shake himself out of his malaise but it was no use. In the account of local historian Ferrar Fenton, at one stage Tate did manage to gather together his forces. He was now ready and prepared to advance on Fishguard but rather than face the British, Fenton states, the men of the Legion Noire refused to move.[11]

Fenton's account is interesting, but in all probability is also highly romanticised. According to St Leger and Morrison, Tate had already decided to surrender. Why then would he marshal his forces for a last ditch attack? If it was a final attempted throw of the dice, it failed dismally.

An anonymous local rhyme from the time, origin unknown, succinctly sums up the situation, with Tate and Knox both unwilling and unable to make a decisive move to end the impasse:

Tate, safe behind Llanwnda Rocks,

Was not afraid of Colonel Knox;

Knox, safe behind the turnpike gate

Was not afraid of Colonel Tate.

Whatever the identity of the rhymester he certainly seems to have caught the mood of the moment. Once Castagnier had left and once Knox had withdrawn from Fishguard the whole affair turned into what can only be described as a farce. To some extent it was understandable.

The French felt abandoned and without quality leaders to rally them in their hour of need managed to do little more than run around like chickens with their heads cut off. Human nature being what it is, the further away from Fishguard Knox got, the braver he would have become.

So as Knox and the Fencibles headed down the road towards the turnpike at Trefgarne, their courage grew – just as Tates's might have done, had he known of the withdrawal. From those positions both commanders might pose and threaten but both of them proved to have little stomach for the fight that many had been expecting.

That evening, Tate called a conference of his senior officers, the men crowding into the parlour of Trehowel. The Quartermaster passed on the news that while many of the foragers had returned, most of them were drunk and there was no transport available.

The lack of suitable transport was a crucial point. It is doubtful that any of the foragers had even begun to look for wagons and other forms of transport. Released from the bondage of their officers and NCOs their interest lay simply in whatever food and liquor they might find. It meant, of course, that when they did finally return to the campsite the French were empty-handed. No wagons or horses had been brought back and, to make matters worse, provisions were now running dangerously low.

The livestock of the Peninsula had been, literally, wiped out by the ravenous troops and there seemed to be no possibility of anyone uncovering any more. Nobody had thought of harbouring or stockpiling provisions for the future, not enlisted men, not officers either. Now they were paying the price for such lack of consideration and future planning. It was a harsh lesson, one that was to prove ultimately fatal for the Legion Noire.

And so Tate finally made the inevitable decision. As he had already told the Irish officers there was only one option – he would surrender.

Chapter 13

Surrender

At 9 p.m. on 23 February 1797, Tate's second in command, Jacques Phillipe Le Brun, walked into the crowded square of Fishguard town. He was accompanied by Francois l'Hanhard, one of the Legion's two aide de camps and the only one who was able to speak reasonable English. Le Brun carried in his hand a message:

> Sir, the circumstances under which the Body of French Troops under my command were landed at this place renders it unnecessary to attempt any military operations, as they would lead only to Bloodshed and Pillage. The Officers of the whole Corps therefore intimate their desire of entering into a Negotiation upon Principles of Humanity for surrender. If you are influenced by similar Considerations you may signify the same by the Bearer and, in the meantime, Hostilities shall cease.
>
> Health and Respect, Tate, Chef de Brigade.[1]

The letter was a masterpiece of understatement. If Tate did not realise that 'bloodshed and pillage' were what had been happening all day then he was wearing blinkers. However, he was hoping to gain as much as he possibly could by the terms of the surrender and an offer of capitulation now might mean a fair degree of leniency from the British commanders.

In Fishguard Square the two French officers were met by Thomas Williams, the husband of Mary who had been assaulted and raped at Caerlem earlier in the day. The man seemed to have a knack of being in the right place at the right moment in time.

Eager to get involved in what was clearly going to be the final act, Williams conducted the two French officers to the guard-house that had been set up in a house on the square. At the time it was not the public house that we see today but a substantial town dwelling and only later was it converted into an Inn. Tate and the captive officers were to spend time on board a prison hulk called the *Royal Oak*, so it is easy to see where the name of the future public house came from.

If Thomas Williams wanted to be party to the surrender – and it was a fairly reasonable desire – he was to be bitterly disappointed. He never got inside the building.

At the door to the guard house Williams and the Frenchmen were met by Lieutenant Colonel Knox. It was to him that the Frenchmen saluted and surrendered their arms. They were then escorted inside. In an upstairs room Francois l'Hanhard acted as spokesman, telling the assembled British officers that his commander Colonel Tate wished to sue for peace.

Elements of the British relief forces had been in the town for a few hours but Knox, still bridling from his earlier encounter with Lord Cawdor, briskly informed l'Hanhard and Le Brun that he did not hold the ultimate authority. They would have to wait while he went off to find Cawdor. He took Tate's letter and went back outside to look for his superior officers. Behind him the Frenchmen waited, bemused and unsure about what would happen next.

Almost outside the front door of the house Knox immediately ran into Cawdor and Colby. Reading the letter, Cawdor at once grasped its significance and knew that the advantage had now swung his way. Tate had been hoping for favourable terms – among other things a quick return to Brest, paid for by the British government. Cawdor immediately killed all hope of this. He whispered to Colby that he would accept only unconditional surrender and nothing else.

He swept imperiously up the stairs, stormed into the room and informed Le Brun (through l'Hanhard) that he had vastly superior numbers at his command and, more importantly, his forces were increasing by the hour. Knox caught the mood of the moment and shouted that they had at least 20,000 troops at their disposal.[2]

Cawdor shook his head in despair at the outburst. He was intent on impressing the French with his professionalism – he did not need hotheads like Knox behaving like rank amateurs or adolescents.

Cawdor's next utterance displayed his annoyance. Disdainfully he announced that he would give the French until 10 a.m. the following day and if, by then, they had not agreed to his demands, he would attack. Le Brun gazed around at the magnificent display of colourful uniforms worn by the British officers – the Castlemartin Yeomanry, the Pembrokeshire Militia and the Fishguard Fencibles among others – and immediately lost whatever courage he had left.

The room was crowded. Apart from the two Frenchmen, Cawdor, Colby and Knox, there were also Major Ackland, Gwynne Vaughan from the fort – along with his brother Daniel who had now left his barricaded house – and Colonel James of the Cardigan Militia. Private H.L. Williams, who served in the Fishguard Fencibles, states that Lord Milford was also present in the room. This is highly unlikely. Even if he had had the inclination, the weak, insipid and unwell Lord Milford would have been hard pressed to make the journey from Haverfordwest in the time available.

As a humble private in the Fencibles it would have been unlikely that Williams would have been present in the upstairs room. He would have received information about who was there much later in the day at second or even third hand. Apart from anything else he did not write his account of the invasion until forty years after the event and time has a disconcerting habit of playing false with the truth.[3]

David Salmon in an article for the Journal of the Welsh Biographical Society excuses Williams for his error (which was compounded and repeated by Stuart Jones in his seminal account of the invasion written many years later): 'In matters that came under his observation he is accurate, though in other matters he makes a few small mistakes.'[4]

Regardless of who was or was not present, Cawdor was determined to press home the advantage. Summoning pen and paper, he ordered that the two Frenchmen should be detained for the night and watched as they were led away. Then he began to draft his reply to Tate's letter:

Fishguard, February 23 1797

Sir, The superiority of the Force under my Command, which is hourly increasing, must prevent my treating upon any Terms short of you surrendering your whole force Prisoners of War. I enter fully into your wish of an unnecessary Effusion of Blood, which your speedy surrender can alone prevent, and which will entitle you to that Consideration it is ever the Wish of British Troops to show an enemy whose numbers are inferior. My Major will deliver you this letter and I shall expect your Determination by Ten-o-clock, by your officer, whom I have furnished with an escort that will escort him to me without Molestation.

I am, etc, Cawdor.[5]

Major Ackland and a troop of cavalry immediately mounted and rode off with the message. They encountered almost no French soldiers on their trip and eventually presented the letter to Tate in his headquarters at Trehowel. And there, strangely, given the weakness of his position, the colonel decided to consider his options. He would sleep on his decision, he declared, and would send Lord Cawdor his response in the morning.

In reality Tate had no decision to make. He had only one course of action open to him and that was to comply with Lord Cawdor's demands. Consequently, early on the morning of 24 February, he summoned his other aide de camp, Lieutenant Faucon, and presented him with a message for the British commander. It was brief and it was succinct:

The idea of the officers of the French Corps is the same which you have expressed in your letter.

I therefore authorise Lieutenant Colonel Le Brun and Lt Faucon, my ADC, to meet such officers as you will appoint, to treat in the subject of the surrender of the troops in the usual form.

Salut et respect

Tate.[6]

By 9 a.m. Faucon had come down off the Peninsula and made his way to the British headquarters. It was a long and, despite everything, still dangerous walk for the young man who had little or no idea about how he was likely to be received. The approach to the town and the square were full of British soldiers who stared at him with a mixture of alarm and dislike, but it was not long before he was ushered into the presence of Lord Cawdor.

Despite the clear superiority of his position, Cawdor had spent a restless and sleepless night. He was worried by Tate's request to consider the situation in the morning and the British commander must have felt that maybe, just maybe, he had overplayed his hand. Now that the French had agreed to surrender on any terms it was an immense relief for him.

Tate's letter meant capitulation, complete and total. The invasion was over and the British people could breathe easily again. Much of the success was down to him and his actions but Cawdor was not the type of man to revel in his glory. It had been a strange affair, something that the travel writer H.V. Morton later declared had a 'strong flavour of musical comedy about it.'[7]

Hindsight is perhaps the only exact science, but Tate's invasion did not seem like musical comedy at the time. None of the defenders really knew what they were facing and there were moments in the affair when things could easily have gone the other way.

* * *

According to local legend the terms of surrender were drawn up and signed on a table that is still preserved in the Royal Oak public house at Fishguard. That may well be the case but there is no provenance to either prove or disprove the claim; like so many other aspects of the invasion however, it makes a great story.

Tate was not present at the signing and Le Brun and the two aide de camps officiated in his absence. He did, however, sign the document – which has since been lost – at Trehowel later in the day. Losing the surrender document seems, now, to be a fitting end to the invasion, the final cap on what was always something of a hair-brained plan.

The disappearance of the surrender document had no real effect on proceedings as the formal arrangements took place with little or no problem. It is interesting to consider what happened to the document, however. Perhaps it was appropriated by some eager souvenir hunter, but as far as Cawdor and Colby were concerned it did not matter. The French had surrendered, that was the important thing.

For the first time in many days Lord Cawdor could breathe easily. A brief look at his diary shows how fraught the period had been.

Cawdor was normally a regular journal writer and compiler, each day being filled in with records of his activities. The four days before, during and after the invasion scare, however, are totally blank and eager researchers hunting through his papers to find out his feelings and emotions at that time will uncover absolutely nothing.[8] Put simply, Cawdor had more on his mind that filling in the pages of his journal.

If Cawdor and the other commanders were relieved, the people of Fishguard and of Pembrokeshire were overjoyed. They had faced adversity and they had triumphed; now they could once again sleep easily in their beds at night.

If there were lessons to be learned, well, that could happen in the days and weeks ahead. For the French, the salutary lesson could not be postponed. However it was looked at, the result of the invasion was easily seen:-

'The last invasion of Britain was over – – –The three days invasion (22 to 24 February 1797) of the 'Black legion' under Tate, designed by Hoche as the harbinger of an army of liberation, was the greatest fiasco in the entire history of projected invasions against the British Isles. Never was the theory that criminals and jailbirds are revolutionary material exposed as harshly.'[9]

The researcher or historian, the enthusiast or the general reader is still left with one thought – the dreaded question of what if? It had all promised so much and Colonel Tate must have been plagued by so many mixed emotions as he appended his signature to the surrender document. He could and perhaps should have achieved so much more.

* * *

Lord Cawdor might have been relieved but he was also a careful and practical man. He would not rest fully until all of the French invaders were locked up behind bars. Early in the morning of 24 February, long before Faucon arrived with the capitulation, he drew up his troops in line of battle outside Fishguard. From there they could, if it proved necessary, march out onto the Pencaer Peninsula and finish off the clearly demoralised French.

Once Faucon had delivered Tate's message it was an easy matter to move his troops and arrange them in order to receive the surrendering enemy soldiers on Goodwick Sands. The wide expanse of beach and a low tide made it relatively easy to accommodate such a large body of men.

It was crucially important to arrange the victorious army in as advantageous a position as possible. There was still a chance that Tate might change his mind, particularly when he saw how few troops Cawdor had at his disposal. So the British commander knew that he still had to play 'mind games' with his defeated enemy.

The men of the Legion Noire were already demoralised and Cawdor was intent on making them feel even worse. He positioned troops on Bigney Hill and Windy Hill overlooking the beach and with excellent views of the sands and the tiny village of Goodwick. The Yeomanry Cavalry was positioned on Goodwick Bridge while the Fishguard Fencibles and the Cardigan Militia were drawn up on the sands themselves.[10]

The numerical strength of Cawdor's forces was greatly increased by the hundreds of spectators who flocked to witness the event. To anyone standing on Goodwick Beach it must have seemed that the town was defended by a force of many thousands.

The French failed to oblige the eager spectators, however. By midday they had still not appeared and Cawdor began to have doubts about the authenticity of their request to surrender. All of the old concerns and worries returned – what if it had been a ruse and the French were, even now, moving off the Peninsula in the other direction? If that was the case the whole of Pembrokeshire would be open before them.

Cawdor despatched an aide de camp, the same Captain Edwardes who had gone with Colby to Fishguard Fort on the first night, to see what was happening in the French camp. Edwardes was accompanied by two Yeomanry troopers and by a civilian, Mr Charles Millingchamp. In his hand Millingchamp carried a flag of truce.

It must have been a nervous ride for all of them. Here and there they came across small groups of drunken or sleeping Frenchmen. They woke briefly, glared at the riders and then slipped back into unconsciousness. It was disconcerting, but nobody seemed inclined to interfere with their progress.

'Keep your eyes peeled,' Edwardes told the two troopers as his horse skittered and snorted in the breeze.

'You think they'll attack?' Millingchamp asked, his hand hovering above the pommel of his sword. 'I don't suppose we'd have much chance if they did. But will they, that's the question?'

Edwardes shook his head. 'I doubt it. I think most of them are too tired or drunk to bother us. But there could always be some stupid clown who thinks he can still win the war for the revolution!'

When Edwardes and Millingchamp reached the French encampment they found the reason for the delay. The French officers were having a difficult time trying to organise their troops. None of them wanted to move away from their camp fires and their response to orders was surly.

There seemed to be utter chaos in the French ranks, many of the convict soldiers thinking they were being lined up to be shot. No amount of cajoling or ordering seemed able to convince them otherwise.

The appearance of Edwardes and his party, however, seemed to bring some sort of order and, as the British delegation waited impatiently, the men of the Legion Noire were, at long last, brought to their feet. Just after 1.30 p.m. they finally began to march away from the Pencaer Peninsula. According to one observer: 'When the French reached the top of Goodwick Hill, they played their music all the way down to the sands, their brass drums echoing through the hills.'[11]

It was hardly the way Tate had intended the Legion should leave the Peninsula and there was an undoubted mood of sadness in some of the more fervent republicans in the ranks. For the vast majority, however, there was just relief that it was all over. Captivity might have been beckoning but at least it was safe.

Chapter 14

The Aftermath

The first of the French soldiers arrived on Goodwick Sands just after two o'clock. Under the watchful – and still distrustful – eyes of the Fishguard Fencibles they began to pile their arms on the beach, arms which had, in the most part, never been fired in anger. By four o'clock the whole of the Legion was there and bread and cheese were handed out to the prisoners.

This was better than sitting cold and hungry up on the Peninsula, most of the Frenchmen thought, as they tore at the provisions with their hands and teeth. Now that they were safely made captive, the French soldiers did not seem so frightening and the Fishguard Fencibles preened themselves as they patrolled around their beaten enemy.

Their food eaten, Major Bowen and a small detachment of the Pembroke and Fishguard Fencibles brought the prisoners to their feet and marched them away from the Sands. They took the road to Haverfordwest, not that far away as the crow flies but a long enough march for men who were headed towards captivity. None of the French were eager to complete the seventeen-mile journey and they dragged their feet and constantly fell out of line.

In the end the march took ten hours. Bowen kept them going throughout the night, however, and the last of the prisoners arrived in Haverfordwest at 4 a.m. on Saturday.

Those who could be accommodated in the castle gaol of the county town were, perhaps, the unfortunate ones. The gaol consisted of just six dirty, rat-infested rooms which were damp and without heating, lighting or ventilation. In the context of the times, prisons were not intended to be reforming institutions, they were there to punish. Haverfordwest bridewell fitted that aim perfectly.

The vast majority of the prisoners had to be herded into the churches of the town – St Martin's, St Mary's and St Thomas's.[1] The churches were warmer and more welcoming than the bleak, brutal confines of the town gaol. There was also a lot more freedom, no matter how well the churches were guarded and patrolled. And that was not always a good thing.

Over the next few weeks, the damage caused by the prisoners to the interior of St Mary's was proof positive that these recalcitrant Frenchmen were not in any way grateful for the better surroundings of the church. Clearly they needed a firm hand – a sentiment with which Colonel William Tate would certainly have agreed.

Colonel Tate had remained at Trehowel while his Legion was being marched off into captivity. There were many sick and a few wounded to care for, thanks in the main to the after effects of under cooked or raw poultry and too much Portuguese wine. Whether Tate was needed to care for these men is doubtful. More likely he simply could not face the final march of the Legion that he had hoped to take to Liverpool and beyond.

There is a very real possibility that the chef de brigade was suffering from nervous exhaustion. It was not quite a breakdown but he was certainly depressed and heavily stressed, all of his dreams and ambitions having been smashed away like winter frost before the sun. If that is the case it would account for his behaviour during the later journey to London.

While he was at Trehowel waiting for Lord Cawdor to take him into protective custody, a strange encounter took place between Tate and John Mortimer, the owner of the farm house. Choosing this moment to make his return home, Mortimer was met at the door by the French commander. Tate seemed unsure of himself, somewhat lost and without purpose. Nevertheless, he presented Mortimer with his sword and attempted to act with a degree of dignity.[2]

'Are you the master here?' Tate asked.

When Mortimer nodded his agreement Tate responded with the brief comment 'I was once master here as well.'

It must have been something of a disconcerting meeting, the two residents or rulers of Trehowel coming together like this. Despite being shocked and angered by the damage to his house and property, Mortimer was magnanimous in victory. This was the occasion that Tate declared how his heart had failed him the moment he stepped ashore – a somewhat unusual declaration for a man who had come to Britain with the express purpose of fomenting open rebellion.

By now Lord Cawdor had left Fishguard, handing over command of the 'mopping up' operation to Colonel Colby. It was another snub to young Thomas Knox – or at least he took it as such, despite the fact that Colby had always been second in command and was the logical person to finish off the campaign.

Cawdor, once he left Fishguard, rode hard for Haverfordwest, overtaking the long column of prisoners. He had to make arrangements for them, decide where to house them and so on. It was a mammoth task. There were, after all, nearly 1,500 Frenchmen to lodge and imprison, but Cawdor completed the task with his usual skill and efficiency.

The French officers had been separated from the men after the surrender at Fishguard. Once the soldiers were marched away they were taken first to Trehowel where they presumably picked up Colonel Tate. Given horses, they were escorted by Major Ackland and taken, via Camrose, to Haverfordwest. There they were accommodated in a single room at the Castle Inn and settled down for the night in relative comfort.[3]

The French officers may not have exactly sung and danced their way into captivity but with the prospect of hot food and a few bottles of wine, things certainly looked a lot brighter than they had done up on the Pencaer Peninsula. Maybe captivity would not be so bad after all.

* * *

One of the best known and most interesting stories about the invasion – although not necessarily the most truthful – is the legend of the Welsh women and their supposed part in the defeat of the French. According to legend, their role was hugely significant: 'The Welsh women, perhaps, did much better work than the men on these memorable two or three days, for by their red shawls they frightened the enemy immeasurably.'[4]

Lord Cawdor, so the story goes, cleverly arranged for hundreds of local women to line the hillsides so that the French would, from a distance, mistake them for regular British soldiers. In some accounts Jemima Fawr (Jemima Nicholas) was at the forefront of the women.

Dressed in their traditional scarlet or red cloaks and shawls, their heads surmounted by tall black hats and bonnets, the women were duly mistaken for guardsmen. The French then supposedly panicked, and began to believe they were outnumbered by troops of greater quality. The result – surrender!

It is a wonderful story, one that has been advanced and compounded by many writers over the years. Ferrar Fenton, for example, commented that Cawdor ordered the women of the area to line the walls and hills, wearing their shawls and hats. He supplied them:

> with real muskets and bayonets, and others with stakes, pokers and the old fashioned roasting spits ... These brave lasses in their tall steeple-crowned hats would make the French (whom he knew would advance across Goodwick Sands, in the hope that some stores would be found there) believe they were in the face of an overwhelming force.[5]

Fenton writes a convincing story but he then goes on to spoil the effect by declaring that Tate was alarmed when the British soldiers – in reality the women – did not open fire on him as he advanced across the beach. The real British soldiers, Fenton states, had already discharged their first volley. It was, according to Fenton, mostly the confusion and fear surrounding this incident that caused the French to mutiny and surrender.[6]

Fenton's tale is decidedly interesting but it is also decidedly wrong. There are no records of any French advance across Goodwick Sands, nor of shots fired by the British soldiers who were drawn up to meet them. Quite apart from the fact that the French did not leave their encampment except to surrender, any frontal or traditional battle would have been disastrous for Cawdor's tiny force. He was aware of this, one of the reasons he would have resisted coming face to face with the enemy unless all of the other options had been tried and failed.

The story did not die with Ferrar Fenton. The Reverend Daniel Rowlands took it a stage further. According to him, Lord Cawdor, after persuading the women to line up in the manner of regular troops, began to manoeuvre them around. He even ordered them to advance towards the enemy:

> Ere long a sudden dip in the ground rendered them invisible to the French, at which place, turning into a side lane, they came again to the back of the hill where they had started, and renewed their former course. It was done almost in the way, in which I am told, these effects are managed in the theatre.[7]

Long after the dust had settled on the invasion, one of the Fishguard Fencibles, H.L. Williams, produced an account of the affair. While his version of events is not always totally reliable, his book was verified as an accurate telling of the tale by two comrades, also former Fencibles, Peter Davies and Owen Griffith.

In his book, Williams mentions a French lady who, some years after the invasion, visited the site of the camp on Pencaer. During her visit she recounted the story – which she claimed was common knowledge on the other side of the English Channel – of her countrymen being frightened by the red flannel mantles of the Welsh women. She even went as far as to buy one of the scarlet shawls, Williams writes, to take home and taunt the French military.[8]

Alexander Ridgway, grandson of Ensign Thomas Ridgway of the Pembroke Fencibles, wrote about the invasion in an article in 'The Times' published on 23 December 1859. According to him, family legend was clear – Squire or Captain Campbell (Lord Cawdor) made deliberate use of the women watchers:-

> [They] were marshalled in their red whittles or hooded cloaks by Captain Campbell to impose on the French messenger an exaggerated notion of the number of corps opposed to them.[9]

Apart from the singular tense ('messenger' as opposed to 'messengers'), Ridgway cannot be alluding to Le Brun and l'Hanhard as nobody knew they were coming until they arrived in the town square on the evening of 23 February. His reference, therefore, to the 'French messenger' must relate to the arrival of Faucon on the morning of the twenty-fourth. By this time the decision to surrender had already been taken and if the marshalling of the women really did happen then their intervention cannot have influenced Tate's decision to throw himself on Lord Cawdor's mercy.

Or can it? Whether their deployment was as deliberate as Fenton and Rowlands make out remains a matter of conjecture and personal belief. But there is some element of truth in the story.

The French did genuinely believe they were outnumbered; it was an impression that Lord Cawdor, by his own account, took pains to promote. Yet for the legend of the Welsh women to have any real substance the deception must have taken place on the evening of 23 February. Unfortunately for the credibility of the story it was already dark when Cawdor and his forces reached Manorowen at the foot of the Peninsula. Indeed it was the very darkness of the night which forced him to abandon his attack that evening.

In that darkness, and in their physical and emotional state, it is highly unlikely that the French would be able to see real soldiers, let alone women masquerading as troops of the line. By 9 p.m. Tate had made his decision to surrender and despatched Le Brun and l'Hanhard on their peace mission. The following morning Faucon was at the Royal Oak by nine and there was then neither the time nor the reason for Cawdor to implement his ruse.

Lord Cawdor makes no mention of the story in his own account of events, stopping short at his appeals for locals to join his troops. He was clear that he not only wished to augment his force, he also wanted that force to seem as large as possible in order to confuse the French. In that aim he certainly succeeded.

When it came to the surrender on Goodwick Sands, many Welsh women from the town and surrounding countryside would, like their menfolk, have been present as spectators. From a distance cowering, frightened and half-drunk convicts might well have mistaken them for soldiers.

Mistaken they may have been but by then it was already too late to terrify them into surrendering. That decision had already been made. And while Lord Cawdor certainly wanted them there, he did not march them around Bigney or Windy Hill in order to fool the French.

It was not just at the surrender that such a mistake could have taken place. During the long Thursday, as French marauders and foragers were engaged in plundering the cottages of the region they would have seen figures in the distance. They would have noticed them on the adjacent hills, on the roads and tracks, either standing silently and watching or streaming away towards Haverfordwest. The women would have been dressed in their red shawls and it is possible that the drunken Frenchmen mistook their movements for soldiers deploying.

The earliest mention of the story can be found in a letter from a man called John Mathias to his sister Mary Harry who was in service with a family at Swansea. Dated 27 February, just three days after the surrender, the letter reads as follows:

Dear Sister

I write to you hoping that you are in good health as I am at present, thanks be to God for it. The French invaded near Fishguard last Wednesday which put the County in great confusion because they wear [sic] 14 hundred … The County gathered from all parts of Pembrokeshire near four hundred women in red flanes and Squier [sic] Campbell went to ask them were they to fight and they said they were and when they came near the French put down their arms and they was all took prisoners and were brought to Haverfordwest Friday night last. We had no more than about four hundred men under arms and they thought the women to be a Ridgment [sic] of Soldiers.[10]

Interestingly, the letter, couched in phrases and sentences that must have come hard to a man not used to putting pen to paper, does not credit Cawdor (Squier Campbell as he is called) with deliberately trying to deceive the French. Mathias simply says that Cawdor asked the women if they would be willing to fight and that they promptly agreed.

It is an intriguing picture – Cawdor, still the man of the people despite his recent ennoblement, trotting across to the various groups of women as they waited for the French to attack. He would have spoken to them in words they understood, just like they understood the seriousness of the situation, and they responded brilliantly. The fact that the French mistook them for guardsmen or, as John Mathias has it, 'A Ridgment of Soldiers', was their own mistake.

A further account of misunderstanding can be found in *Chambers Journal of Popular Literature* for 1860. With regard to the French belief that they were outnumbered, the anonymous author remarks:

> Preparatory to his contemplated attack on the Frenchman's stronghold, Lord Cawdor rode out, at the head of his Yeomanry, to within half a mile of their camp. Had the enemy been furnished with artillery, as their lofty rock commanded the road, they need not have left alive one single horseman back the news of his comrades fate. As it was, after a careful survey, the party coolly trotted off homewards.

> This visit, curiously enough, led to important results. The French officers, deceived by the splendid chargers and handsome uniforms of these forty yeomen, mistook them for the English general and his staff; and presuming that so large a military suite must belong to a proportionately large body of troops, it was resolved to treat for surrender.[11]

Here, perhaps, there is a nucleus of truth and also, perhaps, the origin of the legend about the Welsh women. Some of the detail is clearly wrong; the incident could not have happened on the morning of the surrender but it might well have taken place the previous day. Lord Cawdor, accompanied by his Yeomanry Cavalry, had gone forward to scout out the situation while the two elements of his force – the men from the south and the Fishguard Fencibles – were resting at Trefgarne.

Bearing in mind that the members of the Castlemartin Yeomanry were all men of some substance, it would be logical for them to have horses of grace and style. Their uniforms, while principally blue, were still rather flamboyant and extravagant. The writer was, perhaps, not far off the mark when he states that the French mistook the horsemen for the staff of the British general.

Tate had already witnessed the skirmish between his men and Whiteside's sailors earlier in the day. If he was not on the heights of Carn Gelli when Cawdor approached he would almost certainly have been summoned by St Leger or one of the other officers as Cawdor and his cavalry approached. If he really did believe that he was seeing the staff of a very large army then there is no wonder that he began to panic.

Taking all this into consideration, along with many sightings of the red-cloaked women, it is easy to see how the story of deception began to gain credence. Add in other elements from earlier in the story – the blank shot fired from Fishguard Fort, John Owen's statement that 500 troops of the line defended the town – and it all helps build the story of Cawdor's deception and the legend of the Welsh women.

What is patently untrue is the version of Lord Cawdor marching his phantom army, Jemima Nicholas in the van, around a hill in a deliberate ploy or ruse. That story owes more to the 'fiction' of Ferrar Fenton and the Reverend Rowlands than it does to the truth.

And yet the legend has survived and even grown in popularity. When the centenary of the landing was celebrated in 1897 a huge parade marched from Fishguard to Careg Wastad Point. A prominent part of the parade consisted of women dressed in the traditional national costume of Wales. Even the tapestry commemorating the bi-centenary in 1997 takes a traditional view, with Jemima and her women occupying a central position.

There is no doubt that local women played a highly significant part in the defeat of the French. But so too did the men of the town. Without the active participation of both groups the outcome would have been very different indeed.

* * *

Tate and his men were now in captivity but what happened to Commodore Castagnier and the four ships that had delivered the Legion to Fishguard is another story. In its own way it is just as fascinating and just as misguided as the history of Colonel Tate and his Legion.

On leaving the Welsh coast, Castagnier had proceeded – in line with his out of date instructions – to the Dublin roads. The original aim of such a manoeuvre was to support the French operation in Ireland and to prevent any British relief force from landing. As a plan it was totally reasonable – as long as there was a French presence in Ireland.

Hoche's adventure to Ireland had come to grief several months before, but nobody had even considered changing the commodore's instructions. There was no point in the French fleet heading for the Dublin roads and Castagnier was merely wasting his time off the Irish coast. He was also placing himself and his squadron in terrible danger.

It is hard to see what was going through Castagnier's mind as he paced his quarterdeck and watched his fleet patrol the waters outside Dublin. He, like Tate, would have known that the French expedition to Ireland had failed and that his orders should have been changed. He was in charge of a valuable squadron of new ships but it was a squadron that could serve no purpose by sailing easily along the Irish coast.

His actions, however, have to be looked at in the context of the time. The terror of the Jacobins was still recent enough to frighten anyone in charge of military operations and it was more than probable that Castagnier was sticking rigidly to his instructions, wrong-headed as they might be, simply because he had neither the will nor the courage to change them. It was clearly not the time for individual thought and deed.

To begin with Castagnier's luck held. He was not intercepted and he encountered no enemy warships. Soon after leaving Fishguard the lugger *Vautour* was detached from the squadron and sent off to Brest with news of the successful landing in Wales. Inevitably, given his frame of mind, Castagnier's part in the operation was carefully embroidered.

More important than that, when the *Vautour* reached Brest safely she brought with her much needed information for the admiral, Morard de Galles. Tate might well have landed but as far as the admiral was concerned Castagnier's success in putting him ashore meant simply that the commodore was on his way back to France and he was coming with three valuable and much needed warships.

Three frigates (and the lugger *Vautour*) might appear to be a rather small number of ships but the French navy had only recently achieved numerical superiority over the British. That was something Morard de Galles and the Directory did not want to lose. Tate and his sad blackguards were clearly expendable; the frigates were not.

Meanwhile, still cruising off the coast of Ireland, Castagnier encountered a convoy of small merchant ships. Some accounts put the number of ships in the convoy as high as eleven. However many there were, Castagnier promptly sank them and took nearly 400 prisoners.[12]

Aware that the merchant fleet would soon be missed, Castagnier now headed towards the Scillies in an attempt to throw off any pursuers. There were none and so he simply turned his ships around and sailed back towards the Irish coast. He was now encumbered with many prisoners but he doggedly remained in position. It was a stubbornness or lack of imagination for which the commodore was to pay most dearly.

A sudden storm sprang up when the squadron was off Cape Clear – yet another example of the weather helping Britain defend her coast. The *Vengeance* lost her main yard and shipped 4ft of water in her hold. More significantly, the *Resistance* lost her rudder in the gale. She was out of control and in danger of foundering. Eventually the *Constance* managed to get her in tow and, slowly, the two ships began to head for Brest.

For some reason Castagnier now decided to leave the two battered ships and head for home on his own. Later, Capitaine de Vaisseau Matagne of the *Resistance* was to complain bitterly of being abandoned by his commander. The *Vengeance*, he reported, had repeatedly ignored his requests for a tow and had then deserted him. Castagnier counter charged that the Capitaine had disobeyed his instructions and this was what had led to the damage and, ultimately, to the disaster that was to befall the fleet.

The *Constance* and the damaged *Resistance* limped steadily towards Brest. Unfortunately for the French, Captain Longcroft, the Regulating

Officer in Haverfordwest, had alerted the Admiralty that the French squadron had left Wales and would now be heading for home.

As a result of Longcroft's message, a small British fleet consisting of the *Shannon*, *Beaulieu* and *Mercury* set sail to intercept them. The Spithead Fleet, consisting of many men-of-war, was also now at sea and off Ushant. Sir Harry Burrard Neale was in command of the 36 gun *St Fiorenzo* and the similarly armed frigate *La Nymphe*.

Each and every one of these British squadrons would have been enough to destroy the French ships. If Castagnier had used his judgement and headed for Brest several days earlier he would have avoided them completely. As it was, on 9 March Captain John Cooke on *La Nymphe* spotted the sails of two French warships approaching Brest from the west. Sir Harry Burrard Neale was alerted and the two British vessels cleared for action.

The battle was short and sharp, a running fight which took place within sight of the French coast. Sir Harry's despatch to Lord Bridport sums up the significance of the action: 'With a leading wind out of Brest, and the French fleet in sight from our Tops, it was an object of great importance to be as decisive as possible in our mode of attack.'[13]

Sir Harry was clearly thinking of the morale-value of sinking or capturing the French ships in front of the furious eyes of their compatriots in Brest. The two British vessels closed to within 40ft before opening fire. The effect was devastating on two ships already hindered by storm damage. Neither of the French crews had much stomach for the fight, as Sir Harry was to note:

> As the largest ship was headmost, we both engaged her very warmly ... and compelled her to surrender after a short resistance. By this time the smaller frigate had arrived up, and being attacked by both ships in the same manner as the former, her resistance tho' better made, was not long; she struck her colours at 9.00 a.m.[14]

The whole action had lasted barely half an hour. During the fight the *Constance* lost both her fore and main masts while, on the French ships, a total of eighteen sailors were killed and a further fifteen seriously wounded. No British seamen were killed in the action although there were several injuries.

Once they had struck their colours, both of the French ships were taken in tow and, a few days later with the weather still bad, arrived safely in Plymouth. Sir Harry was more than a little pleased with the captured vessels which brought him and his crews considerable prize money. After commenting on the quality of both French vessels he concluded his despatch with the following, somewhat self-congratulatory words: 'These are two of the Frigates which landed the Troops in Wales. It is a pleasing circumstance to have completed the failure of that expedition.'[15]

There is an interesting, though slight, Pembrokeshire connection in the person of John Cooke, captain of La Nymphe. Commended for his gallantry in the action, Cooke went on to command HMS Belleraphon in Nelson's fleet at the Battle of Trafalgar. He was killed by musket fire during the battle, whereupon his first lieutenant, William Pryce Cumby, took command of the ship and promptly saved her from destruction by hurling a live hand grenade overboard at a crucial stage of the action.

When the Napoleonic Wars reached a conclusion, Cumby was appointed captain superintendent of the new Pembroke Dockyard, a bare thirty miles south of Fishguard. It was an important appointment for the ex-Nelson man but, sadly, Cumby died during his first year in office and was buried in the Pembrokeshire soil that Tate and his Legion had planned to desecrate. His name lives on in a street of the newly created town of Pembroke Dock.[16]

The Resistance was, as Sir Harry Burrard Neale had stated, a fine ship. She was repaired, renamed Fisguard (the old way of spelling Fishguard) and commissioned into the Royal Navy. After an active career which included a famous battle with the Immortalite and being part of the Walcheren Expedition, she was finally broken up in 1814.

The Constance also served in the Royal Navy, although with less success. Her name was not changed – an element, or example, of bad luck, perhaps? In 1810, while engaging a shore battery on the Brittany coast, her captain was killed and she ran aground on the rocks below the battery. She was duly retaken by the French.

And what happened to Castagnier and the *Vengeance*? Like the lugger *Vautour*, the *Vengeance* managed to make port but was captured in 1800 by a British ship in the waters around Jamaica. Despite falling into British hands and being commissioned into the Royal Navy, the damage to her superstructure and hull made it impossible for her to ever sail again.

Little is known about the life and career of Jean-Jeanne Castagnier after he returned to France. He was hugely critical of the *Vengeance*, calling her a monster of a vessel and asking Morard de Galles to give him a new ship. After that he seems to have faded from the pages of history.

If there was any French success in the expedition to Wales, it was surely achieved by Castagnier. He had, after all, sunk somewhere in the region of fifteen enemy merchant ships and completed his mission to land the Legion Noire on British soil. If he had only used his own judgement and not stuck rigidly to his out of date and useless orders he might have gone down as one of the great French warriors of the Revolutionary Wars. He didn't and, as a result, has been condemned to the role of a bit-part player in one of the strangest episodes of the eighteenth century.

Chapter 15

Effects

The effects of Tate's landing at Fishguard were many and varied. Once news of the landing broke there was a fairly understandable panic, particularly in the area around Fishguard and in the rest of Pembrokeshire.

In that initial wave of panic, the first instinct of many was to flee inland, away from the coast and from what most people soon expected to be groups of rampaging Frenchmen. Many of those who fled took their belongings, their riches, even their animals, with them.[1]

Such fear and trepidation were not confined to Fishguard and Pembrokeshire. All over South Wales the immediate concern was that the villainous French would soon be arriving to rape, kill and maim people in their beds. In an age long before mass media provided instant news coverage, fear of the unknown and over-use of the imagination were powerful tools, albeit ones that nobody could control. Panic descended across the nation.

That sense of panic was well fuelled by the 'jungle telegraph', a pulsing rumour-machine that seemed able to spread news faster than any group of despatch riders. The rumours that it spread seemingly had no start or finish, but now they spoke of further landings in other, often disparate, parts of the country.[2] Nobody could quite say where these new landings had occurred but everyone knew that they had taken place.

The panic was short lived, however. Once the initial shock began to wear off, it was replaced by a strange sense of calmness and by a clear sense of outrage. How dare they do this to us, seemed to be the almost universal attitude.

There seems to have been a natural and compelling decision that the only way to cope with this problem was to fight. It was not something that was created and led by the landed gentry and the upper classes; most of them had already run for cover. Rather it came from the ordinary men and women of the country, the common folk who were looked down on by the gentry and whose opinions were rarely, if ever, asked for or listened to.

Cawdor exploited this mood in the people and did so unashamedly during his march to Fishguard. The tactic showed the quality of the man and the result undoubtedly contributed to the French defeat. Before Cawdor or anyone knew it, the desire to fight back had spread like wildfire across the whole of Wales.

It was a seminal moment, one that was not recognised at the time but which was effectively the start of a revolution – albeit not a revolution like the one Tate and Hoche had hoped for. Never again would the people, the ordinary people of the country, be ignored or disenfranchised in the way they had been before. It would take years for such an attitude to become fully formed and there would be many barriers to cross, many setbacks to surmount. But it was the beginning of reform, the start of what really was the rebirth of the nation.

Within hours of the landing, urgent action was being taken. All over Britain, troops were mobilised and many were sent in the direction of Fishguard. The New Romney Fencible Cavalry, for example, was quickly summoned from its base in Worcester and four troops of the Regiment did actually arrive in Pembrokeshire. They may have been too late to take part in the action but they did arrive in time to escort the French prisoners when they were eventually moved from Haverfordwest.

Volunteers flocked to join the various units and even hard-bitten industrialists like Richard Crawshay of Merthyr gathered together bands of workmen and set off to confront the French. It was not long before most of the roads to the west were crammed with baggage trains and hastily armed volunteers, all of them eager to do what they could to combat the outrage that had befallen Fishguard.

News of the surrender, however, halted most of these individuals and makeshift units before they had time to cross the Pembrokeshire border. Many of them, singing and cheering as they marched along the road to the west in what had clearly been seen as something of a 'boys outing', greeted the news with disappointment.

That was how the men of the Carmarthen Yeomanry felt. They had been mobilised as soon as John Vaughan, lord lieutenant of Carmarthenshire, received news of the landing from Lord Milford on 23 or 24 February. The Yeomanry acted swiftly and had reached St Clears on the road to Haverfordwest when an express informed them that their services were no longer required.

It was the same with the Brecon Volunteers who were at Llandovery when they heard the news. Even the Towyn local militia, many miles north of Pembrokeshire, reacted swiftly and units of the regiment were several miles outside town on their way to Fishguard when the story of the French capitulation was announced. Reluctantly, they turned around and headed back home.[3]

With the invasion over and the need for urgent action no longer necessary, fear and anger were replaced by a gruesome curiosity. According to one local legend a clergyman who had been sightseeing at the French encampment climbed down the cliff to where the body of one soldier still lay and cut off one of his fingers. Memento safely in his pocket, the clergyman climbed back up the cliff and went happily on his way. There is no proof that the incident ever happened but the story does reflect the mood of the time.

Another macabre tale concerns the sawn-off ear of a dead Frenchman which was acquired by one family and passed from generation to generation down the ages. Apocryphal, chilling and decidedly weird, the stories of such barbarity do show the curiosity engendered by the invasion – in the wake of the British victory, of course.

A groundswell of rumour and scaremongering persisted long after the French were despatched to prison. Tate's landing, people believed, was merely the first of many such enterprises. As a result, nerves were on edge in a combination of worry and bravado and it was not long before further raids were being reported.

A farmer, John Roach of Llethr in North Pembrokeshire, reported a second landing, just days after Tate had surrendered. He had, he said, heard foreign voices and seen strange ships off the coast. On investigation it was discovered that there were indeed unusual vessels in the area but they were just coastal traders which had put in to land to replenish their water supplies. The alarm had been given however, and John Roach had his moment of glory; for a few days the whole of the county was once more in uproar and forces were gathered to repel this new 'invasion'.[4]

In a country that was well used to seeing ships and sailors of all nations, coastal trading vessels seem to have been the cause of several other reported landings. One of these was at the Worms Head on Gower, another at New Quay in Ceredigion.

Even lieutenant Colonel Knox and the normally reliable Thomas Nesbitt seem to have been taken in by the general mood of alarm. On 6 April 1797 they reported that a fleet of thirteen enemy ships had been sighted off Fishguard. The sole reason for assuming the vessels to be part of another invasion force was that two local vessels had approached the fleet but then quickly tacked around and hurried away.[5]

The fear of another invasion took time to die down. Even news of Sir John Jervis' victory at the Battle of Cape St Vincent failed to dispel all the rumours. The battle had actually taken place on 14 February, just before the French landing at Fishguard, but the news took time to make its way back to Britain and then leak out to the provinces. Even when the story did break it was, to most people, an action that had taken place far away – not like a possible invasion of the home country.

Time was the only healing factor and for Britain, standing alone against the might of Republican France, time seemed to be on the side of the enemy. The naval mutinies at Spithead and the Nore did little to dispel the feeling of insecurity. Small wonder that a frightened, isolated people should resort to rumour and gossip. It was almost all they had.

What ordinary people without any understanding of military tactics and strategy did not understand was the simple fact that small landings with limited numbers of troops and without quick back up or reinforcement were now a thing of the past. Tates' landing had, if anything, proved that to be true.

If there was ever to be an effective invasion of Britain it would have to be organised and carried out on a major scale with vast reserves of manpower and total command, both of the immediate landing area and of the sea. It was something that Napoleon Bonaparte implicitly understood and consequently, following Nelson's defeat of the Combined Fleets at Trafalgar in 1805, he was only too well aware that the chance of a successful invasion of Britain had gone forever.

* * *

At the end of the nineteenth century one of the public's great concerns, right across the country, was the large number of French prisoners of war detained on mainland Britain. There were soldiers and sailors from various regiments and ships, the men being held in prisons, the officers, by and large, in towns where they roamed relatively freely as long as they had given their parole.

None of the prisoners wanted to spend their time in captivity where conditions were far from easy and the thought of home, only a stone's throw away across the Channel, kept constantly intruding on everyone's memory. News of Tate's landing soon reached these disgruntled and disaffected men with the result that a mood of unease began to fall over most of the prison camps.

Housed in gaols like Portchester Castle outside Portsmouth, or sometimes on board prison hulks – old ships, out of commission and rotting quietly, or not so quietly, on the mud of creaks and estuaries around the coast – many of these men were being held close to strategically important sites. For those on or close to the south coast of England the possibility of mass escape and a potential return to France was something that was always in the minds of the authorities.

The release of prisoners of war had been one of Tate's objectives. It never happened, but at Stapleton Prison in Bristol news of the landing brought open rebellion. The militia unit that normally guarded the prisoners had been marched off towards Pembrokeshire to help in the defence of the country. They were replaced by willing but untrained and not very efficient volunteers.

When a riot broke out, the guards had little idea of how to deal with it. In the ensuing chaos one of the volunteer guards shot and killed one of his own men and there were many other injuries on both sides. In another riot at Portchester there was a mass breakout. It was only ended when one of the escaping prisoners was killed.

All over Britain, French officers who had been granted parole began to break the terms of their bail. The government was forced to clamp down on their freedom of movement and this brought further problems. Giving an officer the freedom to move around the town or village – in return for his promise not to attempt an escape – was a relatively easy way of dealing with captured soldiers. To now restrict that movement was costly – both in terms of the number of guards and as an irritant to the French, who resented this sudden clamp-down on their liberty when they had already pledged their word of honour to behave properly.

The question of what to do with prisoners of war became a vexed issue. Should they continue to be held in Britain, fed and clothed at the government's expense? Or should they be sent back to France at the earliest opportunity?

The sudden arrival of nearly 1500 soldiers and convicts in Wales merely added to the problem. The members of the Legion Noire had already displayed their unruly behaviour on the Pencaer Peninsula and in St Mary's Church in Haverfordwest. There was no reason to suppose that they would change that behaviour. As one wit remarked, the British sent their convicts to New South Wales; the French sent theirs to Old South Wales instead.[6]

* * *

Human nature being what it is, it was perhaps inevitable that after such a scare as the invasion of 1797 a witch hunt should begin in Pembrokeshire. People from all walks of life looked around and decided that somebody had to be blamed. In other words, scapegoats needed to be found – if only to ease the consciences of those who had run at the first sight of the French. As far as potential scapegoats were concerned, there were many of them available.

As usual with witch hunts it was the minority groups that suffered most. One of the original aims of the invasion had been to turn the poor, the labourers and peasants of the country, against the rich. The solidarity of the working people, despite their frugal living conditions and despite the gap between the rich and the poor, had been one of the reasons for the failure of the French plan. Therefore, when it came to witch hunts and persecution, there was little mileage in anybody attempting to single out labourers or fishermen from the area for anything but praise.

If scapegoats were going to be found they would have to come from another, perhaps more vulnerable group. The Dissenters and the Nonconformists were an obvious choice.

Two of the first people suspected of helping the French were Thomas Williams of Caerlem and William Thomas of Mathry. Williams was the man who had brought Le Brun and l'Hanhard to the Royal Oak, prior to the surrender. His wife had been shot and raped outside her own home. He would have been an unlikely collaborator but, even so, he was pulled in by the authorities and questioned. William Thomas was a farmer who had lost his watch and silver shoe buckles when he ventured too close to the French encampment. He was a man who would have had little sympathy with the French invaders.

Charges against the two men were soon dropped, not solely because of their activities during the invasion period, but when it was realised that they were both members of the established church, the Church in Wales.[7] Finding nothing suspicious in the behaviour of Williams and Thomas, the search for scapegoats moved on apace.

A Baptist Minister, the Reverend John Reynolds from Solva, had his house ransacked, the searchers looking for a supposed seditious newspaper. Nothing was found and there the matter rested. There were other accusations against Dissenting Ministers and supporters, usually relating to illicit publications, but the perpetrators of the complaints were never identified. As always in such matters, the evil behind the pointing fingers remained in the background.[8]

The Reverend Henry Davies of Llangloffan, yet another Dissenter, was investigated by civil authorities but no charges were ever laid against him. He might have escaped prosecution but feelings against him still ran high and he was burned in effigy at that year's Fishguard Fair.[9]

Three men were finally singled out for punishment – John Reed, a weaver who lived on the Pencaer Peninsula, Thomas John, a yeoman farmer from the Letterston area, and Samuel Griffiths of Poyntz Castle near Brawdy. All three were Nonconformists and in April 1797 all three underwent examination before magistrates in Haverfordwest, accused of collaborating with the French.

John Reed never made it to court. The evidence against him was weak and clearly falsified – something that was going to come back and haunt the prosecutors in the other cases. Consequently, he was bailed and charges against him were dropped.

Thomas John was dealt with first. Accused of giving information about the strength of the defenders, it was reported that he had been seen in the French camp, talking to enemy officers. Unfortunately for the prosecution, one of their principal witnesses was an American sailor by the name of Charles Prudhomme who had served with the Legion, and he later admitted that he had been promised sixty guineas to give false evidence.

Samuel Griffiths, when his turn came, was reported to have told the ADC Francois l'Hanhard that the British forces were small in number and that many of the supposed soldiers were in fact women. Like John he had been seen in the French ranks and had also been seen going in and out of the enemy headquarters at Trehowel.

Despite the flimsy evidence and the fact that it relied solely on the evidence of men like Prudhomme and l'Hanhard, it was decided that there were indeed charges to be answered. Both John and Griffiths were locked up to await the next Quarter Sessions. A long wait beckoned, as those forthcoming Quarter Sessions lay six months in the future.

Conditions in their cells must have been appalling, but the wait did at least give the Frenchmen time to consider their situations and to weigh the validity of their evidence. They admitted that they had perjured themselves and all charges against John and Griffiths were dropped.

Even though the payment of rewards for a conviction was common practice in those days, there had clearly been conspiracy at work. However, nobody was ever charged or accused of attempting to pervert the course of justice. Whoever was behind the false accusations was unknown at the time and remains so even today.

It is perhaps simplistic to say that the accused men were hounded and imprisoned solely because they were Nonconformists. And yet there was considerable strength of feeling against the Dissenting sects, the Methodists in particular. The Duke of Rutland, a pillar of the established church, visited Haverfordwest and its gaol at this time. His comment on what he saw there was short and to the point:

> This part of the country is very much under the influence of the pernicious doctrines of Methodism … They are deceitful in their manners and, under the mask of religion, with piety and meekness in their mouths, they are pests to the community.[10]

Ferrar Fenton was later to claim that Jones and Griffiths had indeed been seen in and around the French camp but that there was nothing traitorous in their actions. They were there, he claimed, because of the natural inquisitiveness of what he called 'the low Welsh'.[11]

The two men could, of course, have been guilty as charged, but it is unlikely. A more acceptable rationale is the lack of religious toleration, particularly from members of the establishment, towards the Dissenters and Nonconformists – who, it must be admitted, viewed the established church and its adherents with a similar degree of dislike.

* * *

From a military perspective there were several positive results of the invasion scare. Ludicrous as the invasion may have been, the French did actually manage to land troops on the British mainland. Had they been troops of quality the damage could have been enormous. There was no way that Cawdor's valiant amateurs could have stood for a moment against battle hardened French regulars and veterans. It was a fear that was too close for comfort.

Following the invasion there was an immediate reappraisal of the country's defences. By and large they were found to be woefully inadequate. Distant regions like Pembrokeshire had never been considered to be in need of serious defence – despite the fact that Milford Haven was one of the finest natural harbours in the world.

When war broke out between Britain and France in 1756, Lieutenant Colonel Bastide of the Royal Engineers surveyed the waters of the Haven and decided that six forts and gun batteries were required to properly defend the area. It seemed little enough to keep safe an area that had seen both Owain Glyndwr and Henry Tudor first come ashore there.

Due to the costs involved, however, this plan was soon reduced to just three forts at the seaward end of the estuary and land was actually purchased in order to build them. By 1759 however, all danger of invasion had passed and none of the forts were ever completed, although the land remained in government hands. It meant that for the rest of the century there was no military defence work of any substance between St David's Head and Cardiff.[12]

Apart from some defence works along the south coast of England and around the mouth of the Thames area, it was the same story right across Britain. The lack of defences and of preparedness was, quite simply, shocking. Nobody, in times of peace, had thought about defending the country – in times of war it was a totally different matter.

The performance of the Royal Navy, the traditional buttress upon which Britain's defence rested, had not been particularly impressive during the invasion scare – at least not until the end of the expedition. It had taken Lord Bridport a week to mobilise and put to sea and had it not been for the ubiquitous frigates, the jacks of all trade, Castagnier's fleet would have got safely home.

The issue was debated in Parliament, a heated and argumentative session, and a heightened sense of awareness regarding the defence of Britain began to permeate government circles. There was much that needed to be done.

Clearly the navy needed more ships. Warships remained Britain's best means of defence and as a consequence several new dockyards, in order to build and repair them, were established. As far as Wales was concerned, a yard was created at Milford in 1802 and transferred up river to Paterchurch Point (later Pembroke Dock) twelve years later.

A dockyard at Malta was opened in 1800 to cater for the vessels of the Mediterranean Fleet. New slipways were provided for yards like Woolwich, Deptford and Portsmouth, and a general upgrading of shipbuilding facilities began to ensure, once and for all, the supremacy of the Royal Navy.[13]

Martello Towers and gun platforms were built along the southern coast of Britain and a system of warning beacons – reminiscent of those used to alert the country of the coming of the Spanish Armada in 1588 – established in various coastal regions. Orders were given for the North Forland, Oxfordness and Harwich lights to be extinguished to prevent enemy ships sailing easily up the Thames and Medway. The Nore buoy was also ordered to be sunk – anything to hinder enemy navigation.[14]

Artillery and ammunition were promised to strategically important towns like Swansea and Bristol – although, in the event, the people of Swansea had to wait until 1803 before their guns arrived.

Perhaps more importantly, recruitment to the various militia and volunteer regiments received a massive boost in the wake of the invasion, thousands of fit and able young men flocking to the colours to 'do their bit'. Should the French attempt to come again they would find Britain much better defended.

The threat of invasion remained strong, however; only Nelson's victory at Trafalgar finally ended the possibility. For several years it seemed likely that Bonaparte would attempt to replicate Tate's landing, albeit with many more troops and much better planning. Lord Nelson, of course, ended that particular dream.

Despite all the promises, defence works took a long time to arrive, with government pledges far outstripping the practicalities of the situation – witness the slow arrival of the guns at Swansea. It was the middle years of the new century before Milford Haven and the extensive new dockyard at Pembroke Dock were given adequate defences. Ultimately, over fifteen forts and gun batteries were to line the Haven but it had been a long time coming.

* * *

The two strongest, or most long-lasting, effects of the French invasion of Fishguard, however, were not military at all. And they were certainly not what General Hoche and the Directory had intended when they appointed Tate to lead the expedition.

If the invasion achieved anything it had to be in the destruction of whatever remnants of radicalism were stored in the hearts and minds of the British. Robespierre and the Terror had cured many of them of their initial interest in and support for the ideals of the French Revolution; the landing in Fishguard merely finished it off:

> The Methodists in particular were now strengthened in their opposition to radicalism. They had been unjustly accused of fomenting riots against conscription in 1795 in Denbeigh and elsewhere, whereas, in fact, they were extreme conservatives in politics. Their belief in predestination paralysed any inclination they had towards reform, and their conviction that the world was but a place of trial in preparation for the afterlife led them to teach that everyone should be satisfied with their lot.[15]

It was not just Methodists. All of the Dissenting sects – many of which had been viewed most suspiciously by the government and by the general public as well – were now united in their desire to defend Britain. The sense of outrage that had followed the 1797 landings built and grew to create a sense of unity in the country that has probably only been matched by the 'fight them on the beaches' attitude of 1940.

Pitt and his government might still be criticised in Parliament and in the press but now such critical reproach was strangely positive.

It came because the invasion had been allowed to take place rather than as a condemnation of the long and costly war itself.

The second major effect lay in the devious and labyrinth channels of finance and money-making. Despite everything, there was no doubt that the invasion took place at a most inopportune time for Pitt's government. They had already made large loans to Britain's allies in a desperate attempt to harden their resolve and shore up their faltering opposition to republican France. As a consequence, cash reserves in the Bank of England were frighteningly low.

Small country banks invariably took their lead from the central organisation and now, sensing trouble ahead, many of them began to withdraw their cash deposits from the Bank of England. 'Better to keep our money in our own vaults where we can see it', was the general theme.

When news of the French landing broke there was a sudden and dramatic run on the banks as hundreds of investors rushed to protect their money in the best way possible – by holding it to their bosoms. The French were coming to rob, pillage and steal, people thought, and the performance of the Legion Noire up on the Pencaer Peninsula seemed to prove them right.

Therefore, it was much safer to take whatever money they had and hide it – bury it in the garden, put it under the bed or plaster it up in a wall alcove. It might not be earning interest but at least it was safe.

Up until then, Bank of England stock had held up reasonably well, particularly during the most recent crisis, when the French had appeared off Bantry Bay late the previous year. But now a mood of panic descended across the country and this time the effect was to be far more dramatic – and far more troublesome for the bank.

On Saturday 25 February, the day after news of the invasion was received in government circles in London, the bank stock slumped four and a half points. The previous day, something of a 'Black Friday' for the British banking industry, there had been an unprecedented withdrawal of cash from the Bank of England and from many of the small country banks as news of the invasion leaked out and frightened investors began to react.[16]

Why the arrival of 1,400 members of the Legion Noire should cause more concern than the huge numbers of soldiers present at Bantry Bay remains a mystery. They had, arguably, managed to get ashore – which was more than Hoche ever achieved – and, of course, this was mainland Britain rather than Ireland. The main reason for the panic was probably that this was the second incursion inside three months and people were worried that yet another landing could take place at any time.

Panic has a habit of creating panic. Once the initial fear forced the first investors to withdraw their money others quickly followed suit – and then more. Soon the fear of losing hard earned savings and capital investments had become an end in itself. The reason now did not matter; the only concern was the burning desire to protect investments.

On that Saturday, Prime Minister William Pitt was approached by two of the Directors of the Bank of England. They were anxious and concerned about the situation and warned Pitt that they did not know how much longer the bank could go on issuing cash payments. This was both a shock and a potential disaster for the government.

William Pitt, normally so cool and collected, began to panic, just like the bankers. The king was called back from his weekend stay in the country and a meeting of the Privy Council took place on Sunday 26 February. They had to find a solution to a problem that was quite likely to bring down the government – and even see the country descend into anarchy.

The following day, cash payments were suspended by the Bank of England. The notice of intent was as straightforward and revolutionary as bankers could make it:

> The Governor, Deputy Governor and Directors of the Bank of England, think it their duty to inform the proprietors of bank stock, as well as the public at large, that the general concerns of the bank are in the most affluent and prosperous situation, and such as to preclude doubt as to the security of its notes. The Directors mean to continue their usual discount for accommodation of commercial interests, paying the amount in bank notes, and the dividend warrants will be paid in the same manner.[17]

For the investors the key was in the last sentence. Not since the Jacobite Rebellion of 1745 had the Bank of England suspended cash payments. This time the suspension and the alternative were long lasting. Instead of coinage, the bank decided to issue notes to the value of £1 and £2, each carrying the promise to pay the bearer the said amount – in effect a government sponsored IOU.

The £2 note soon disappeared from circulation but the £1 variety remained in use and did not disappear until the 1980s, when it was replaced by a £1 coin. That was nearly 200 years after its first issue and nobody at the bank or in government had ever expected it to last so long.

The Bank of England did not resume cash payments for twenty years after 1797 but the bank notes themselves soon became an indispensable part of British life. In the modern world with its credit cards and bank transfers, cheque books and cash dispensers, it is easy to forget the importance that was placed on coinage in the eighteenth century, when only gold or silver – and the land he owned – gave a true reflection of a man's worth. The paper notes issued after 1797 obviously had no value but it was what they represented that was important – and all because of a few French convicts landing in Fishguard.

In the immediate period after the decision was taken to suspend cash payments, the situation remained desperate. If people had refused to take the notes and demanded their money in coinage and cash there would have been an immediate halt in the working of the country.

Eventually it was the support of the London merchants that saved the day. They decided that they would accept the promissory note as payment for goods and other dealings – a significant degree of support for Pitt's government. Had the merchants refused to accept and use the notes there would have been chaos. Riots and rebellions would surely have followed.

A 'knock on' effect took place all over Britain with local merchants and traders also agreeing to the use of the Bank of England notes. A major financial and constitutional crisis had been avoided.

A Select Committee was speedily appointed to examine the affairs of the Bank of England. The result was a report showing that demands on the bank on 25 February 1797 were £13,770,390. To meet these demands the bank had funds of £17,597,280 as well as being owed an additional £11 million by the government. It was tight, but clearly there was more than enough cash in reserve to cover the problem.[18]

Investors did not have any idea of the bank's assets, they were concerned only with their own pools of money. Had the run on the bank continued, such funds would have been quickly eroded as the public continued to demand its money. There was no doubt that Pitt and his government had been badly shaken – but they had survived.

Chapter 16

Players Departing the Stage

Following his defeat, Colonel Tate was dispirited and demoralised. He spent his first night of captivity with his officers in the locked room of the Castle Inn at Haverfordwest. The others might have been happy and relatively contented, but Tate was solemn and withdrawn. He knew that a period of long confinement awaited him.

The following day he and his officers, forty-five of them, were sent on towards Carmarthen. There they were lodged in the Ivy Bush Inn, the most prestigious hotel in the market town. To begin with they were all awarded considerable freedom and, having given their parole, were allowed to wander the streets. Tate as the chef de brigade must have been the subject of considerable interest from the locals but, at this stage, there was remarkably little animosity or anger shown towards him.

It was not too long, however, before problems began to arise. The Mayor of Carmarthen found it necessary to write to the Duke of Portland, the Home Secretary, stating that if the prisoners were to be allowed to roam the streets of the town much longer 'inevitable ruin must follow'.[1] The French officers were being quartered and fed at the expense of the townsfolk and many of them were living very well indeed.

As reports of further French landings began to come in, false as they may have been, the prisoners were hastily moved into the County Gaol. After their relatively comfortable existence in the Ivy Bush, the gaol must have come as something of a shock to the French officers and they were not best pleased with their new quarters.

Lieutenant General James Rooke, officer commanding the Severn District – which included both Pembrokeshire and Carmarthenshire – arrived in the area at this moment. He had come to take command of the operation but found that everything was well in hand and all there was for him to do was to oversee the 'mopping up' that had recently begun.

Rooke must have passed Tate and his officers in Carmarthen but he was headed for Haverfordwest and had no time to spare. At this stage he had little or no idea of what would be facing him. However, finding matters well in control in Pembrokeshire, he and Lord Cawdor soon took the road back to Carmarthen. It had been decided that Tate should be taken to London for examination. With him were to go Phillipe Le Brun, his second in command, and the three Irish officers. Lord Cawdor was to act as their escort.

Early on the morning of 2 March, while most of the town was still asleep, Tate and the others were bundled into a convoy of three carriages. The horses were whipped up and soon Carmarthen lay far behind. In contrast to their earlier sojourn, their last night in the town had been a disturbed one.

Firstly, Cawdor had been alerted of a new landing on Gower. It was a false alarm, of course, but he had spent a few troubled hours pacing the dining room floor and planning how he was going to deal with his charges in light of this new incursion. Then there was a real problem, a serious fire breaking out in the town. As a consequence Cawdor was tired and dishevelled as he and the captives set out on their journey. He was, however, pleased to be on the way.

Cawdor was accompanied by his ADC Joseph Adams of Holyland and by Lord Edward Somerset, ADC to General Rooke. Their way lay along the coach road to Llandeilo, through Brecon and Gloucester and thence to Oxford and, eventually, London.

Cawdor later recalled the journey in a letter to his wife, written once they had reached the capital and taken up lodgings in Oxford Street:

Monday, March 13th 1797

I have at length the satisfaction of an hour's free time from interruption to give you a short account of our employment

etc since I quitted you, but shall reserve much of the detail
for your amusement when we meet.

Jos Adams had charge of Tate and Captain Tyrrell, the first
alarmed and confused, the second a stupid Paddy. I had Le
Brun with me, as dirty as a pig, but more intelligent and
better manners. In the last Lord Edward Somerset had care
of Captain Norris and Lieutenant St Leger, both greatly
frightened – they had but little conversation.[2]

Cawdor has mistakenly called Morrison by the false name of Norris.
Finding out the names of the invaders had been a problem. In the main
they had only the prisoners' words to go on and, sometimes, mistaken
identity overrode everything.

Lord Milford believed that Tate was actually an English criminal
by the name of Wall. This man had been Governor of Senegal where
he had ordered one of his soldiers, a sergeant who was demanding
arrears of pay, to be beaten – and beaten so severely that the man died.
The flogging had been carried out by two black slaves, something that
horrified the British public as much, if not more, than the brutality of
the punishment.

Wall had also killed a friend in a duel and assaulted a lady to whom
he had been betrothed. Brought back to England to stand trial, Wall
managed to escape and fled to the continent where he was popularly
supposed to have joined the ranks of the French army. His infamy was
so widely known that Milford was not alone in his assumption about
Tate. Many of the people Cawdor and his convoy passed on the way to
London believed that the leader of the Legion Noire and the outlaw to
be one and the same man. And they reacted accordingly.

In several places clods of earth were hurled at the prisoners and the
press of people against the carriages was so great that they were brought
to a halt. Lord Cawdor did well to stop his charges being pulled out and
strung up there and then.

In his subsequent letter to his wife Cawdor reported how serious
things had become during the journey, where the open-hearted

acceptance of the prisoners experienced by Tate and the others at Carmarthen had now altered radically: 'At Uxbridge the rage of the mob was chiefly directed against Tate, who was supposed to be Wall, and he trembled almost to convulsions.'[3]

Tate hardly helped himself during the journey. Old and frail, dressed in his blue coat and white waistcoat – complete with the National Cockade of Republican France on his lapel – he trembled constantly and had little interest in the countryside they passed through. He seemed to have lost all heart and when the carriages were surrounded by the angry populace eager for his blood, he cowered away in terror. He had never, not even for a moment, expected or understood the fury of the English mob. To be confused with a monster like Wall (who was later arrested and executed for his crimes) only made matters worse.

London was reached on 4 March when, by cutting through the Park, they managed to reach the residence of the Duke of Portland without too much interference from the crowd. Tate was worried and unsure about his fate. He had no desire to be sent back to the USA. He was, after all, an American citizen and it was against the laws of the United States to engage in acts of war against any country with which the US was at peace. That included Great Britain.

Le Brun was clear about his position, knowing that as a French officer who had done no more than carry out his duty, he would be detained as a prisoner of war. The three Irishmen, however, were in a perilous position. They had waged war against King George and the prospect of trial and execution for treason was quite likely.

The prisoners were taken to the Admiralty where they were examined before a Privy Councillor, Richard Ford, who was also a Bow Street Magistrate. He wrote down their depositions, the Irishmen in particular taking pains to stress that they had no idea their destination was to be Britain. They claimed to believe that they were bound for the West Indies or Dunkirk, presumably thinking – or, at least, pretending to think – that an attack on British Colonies was different from an attack on the British mainland itself.[4]

Only Barry St Leger made no comment about their destination. Perhaps he was more realistic and knew that any denial would be treated with the contempt it deserved. Maybe he was fatalistic – what would be, would be.

In the end it was decided not to proceed with charges of treason against the three Irishmen. The reason for this seeming act of charity was that many Royalists in France, who were working for the British government, or at least against Republican France, would then be liable to the same treatment. The Irish officers would, instead, be detained as prisoners of war.

As for Tate, he was allowed parole – but there was soon a reappraisal of the whole parole situation. It was, the government decided, foolish and short sighted to allow bonded prisoners almost total liberty simply because they had vowed not to escape. It was inevitable that some of these men would break their parole but, more importantly, far too many French officers were wandering at will all over the nation's capital, watching and garnering information that might, one day, be useful to the French military.

As a result, in May 1797, just three months after he had surrendered, William Tate was sent to the prison ship *Royal Oak* in Portsmouth harbour. The three Irishmen went with him.

Conditions on board the prison ships were appalling. Overcrowding was habitual, so much so that many of the French believed it was a deliberate policy from their captors. Prisoners were often forced to sleep on the bare deck and when hammocks were available, only 6ft per person was allowed to sling them. In the summer the ships were hot, sweaty and foul with disease. In winter things were not much better as prisoners, many without proper clothing, froze and shivered in the bitter winds that seemed to be constantly whipping up and down the muddy estuaries where the hulks lay.[5]

There were over thirty prison hulks in use at this time and the *Royal Oak* was no easier or more comfortable than any of the others. Arguably, it was actually worse:

A certain Jean Maneaux on board the 'Royal Oak' … was suspected of giving information to the authorities of an intended escape. His comrades tied him up and thrashed him with a rope's end to which a piece if iron had been attached. When he succeeded in bursting the cords which bound him, they jumped on him until his neck was broken, cut up the body into small pieces, and threw them overboard.[6]

Life on board the *Royal Oak* was probably not always quite so deadly, but it was far from being a place of sanctuary. Tate and the others must have shuddered and wondered what they had come to, particularly after their time in comfortable hotels in Haverfordwest and Carmarthen.

They were soon joined by several more of the officers from the Legion Noire. Some of them apparently brought women – their 'wives' – along with them. At least four women had been on the roll of the Legion Noire although what their purpose actually was has never been clear. Washerwomen or wives, it hardly mattered now. With the total lack of privacy and human dignity on board the *Royal Oak* the women cannot have had an easy time of it.

Desperate to escape such a hellhole, Tate proposed a scheme whereby he might be allowed to go to France on parole. In exchange for his freedom he would negotiate the release of Sir Sidney Smith, the famous frigate captain who, for some time now, had been making life very difficult for French traders and merchant sailors. Smith had recently been captured but much as they admired his prowess and wanted him back on the scene, the response of the British government to Tate's offer was an emphatic 'No, thank you!'

A little later in the year, however, Tate was moved from the *Royal Oak* and lodged in nearby Portchester Castle. Barry St Leger accompanied him to his new place of confinement. Here at last, in the massive old fortress outside Portsmouth, Tate and St Leger were granted a degree of dignity, if not freedom. Living conditions were almost humane and prisoners spent their days gambling, making prisoner of war models out of bone or straw and just thinking and talking about home.

During his confinement Tate witnessed the British naval mutinies at Spithead and the Nore. He fumed at the opportunity that had suddenly presented itself to the French – if only they had known of the British problems. It was another opportunity missed, for when the mutinies were suppressed, the men's grievances dealt with, the Royal Navy was stronger and more efficient than ever.

Tate remained a prisoner for just over a year; on 24 November 1798 he was suddenly sent back to France. It was part of an exchange deal for British sailors and Tate happily seized the opportunity. He set up home – apparently with a woman friend – at the Hotel Boston on the Rue Vaugirand in Paris. He was happy enough, but the Ministry of War seemed unwilling or unable to recognise his rank and it took several months of letter-writing and interviews before he was finally awarded a pension of 1,500 francs a year.

That was not the end of the old warrior, however. Over the next few years he submitted several ideas to the War Department, including a new type of war engine for use against the British. None of them were ever taken up and were probably discarded as the deluded ramblings of an old and disappointed man.[7]

Fifteen hundred francs was little enough to live on and by 1809 Tate's debts stood at between nine and ten thousand francs. A police dossier was opened on him but somehow they were paid off – probably by the efforts of friends and old colleagues. Tate and his lady friend continued to live beyond their means and eventually the American Ambassador intervened. In April that year Ambassador Armstrong contacted Tate and told him that a vessel was about to leave Dunkirk, bound for the USA.

War between the USA and Britain was imminent and so Tate applied to Comte d'Hunebourg, Minister of War, for leave to sail for America. He wanted, Tate said, to contribute whatever he could to the American war effort. In truth the Directory was probably glad to see him go and permission was duly granted. The only drawback was that he would have to forfeit his half-pay salary. It was a price that William Tate, unhappy and disgruntled, was more than willing to pay.

Tate set out from Dunkirk and there he disappeared from the pages of history. Whatever his age, he was unwell and the rigours of such a trip cannot have been easy for a man who had seen and done so much.

It is not known if he reached America but, hopefully, he made it back to his homeland. It was the least he deserved.

* * *

General Lazarre Hoche, the man behind the invasion plan, was posted away from Brest before Tate and his Legion ever left the port. Sent to the Low Countries of Holland and Belgium, the little general found himself in considerable disfavour with the Directory. After all, his grand plan to land an army in Ireland, along with Quantin's attack on Newcastle, had come to nothing and nobody really had much faith in Colonel Tate and the Legion Noire.

Then, suddenly, in September 1797 Hoche died. Officially the cause of death was consumption and there is no doubt that years of campaigning in all types of weather had adversely affected his health. There were rumours, however, that he had been poisoned, whether by the enemies of Republican France or by factions within the army has never been made clear.

It is difficult to say, with any real certainty, what happened. What is for sure is that with the death of Hoche, the Directory lost its foremost soldier. It meant that when Napoleon Bonaparte staged his coup d'état a few years later there was nobody with the courage or the skill to oppose him. Had Hoche still been around the course of European history might well have been very different.

Lieutenant Colonel Le Brun and most of the other officers from the Legion Noire, French and Irish alike, were repatriated to France at about the same time as Tate. In the main they were exchanged for British captives like Sir Sidney Smith.

The only exception was Barry St Leger. Always the best of a bad bunch, St Lager planned, plotted and schemed, waiting his time. He was ready for the opportunity that he knew must, one day, come his way. In due course it did. Somehow St Leger managed to escape from Portchester Castle and disappeared from the scene. There remains, however, a small footnote: twenty years later the widow of Sir Edward Mansell, a soldier with several Pembrokeshire connections, married a

Colonel Barry St Leger – of the British, not the French, army. Whether or not it was the same man who had striven so gallantly to make the invasion a success is not known. It would make a fine ending to his story if it could be proved to be true.[8]

The majority of the Legion, the rank and file plus one or two junior officers remained for a while in Haverfordwest. When they had left Trehowel and the Pencaer Peninsula they had left behind tons of ammunition and stands of muskets. They also left twenty-eight wounded and sick comrades. Lieutenant Colonel Knox, left to clear up things around the farm house, allowed the ill men to remain at Trehowel for the first night after the surrender but the following day they, along with the ammunition, were loaded into hay carts and sent off to join their comrades in Haverfordwest.

The Legion Noire might have gone, but Fishguard and the surrounding area remained full of British troops. There was always, at least in the minds of the military planners, the fear that the French would return in even greater numbers. They did not come again but there was to be another fatality in the town. Captain Edwardes was soon reporting:

> I have to lament an accident which happened this morning by the firing off of a pistol by one of the Pembroke Yeomanry, the contents of which lodged in the abdomen of a woman. It is not yet ascertained whether the wound is mortal or not though I am rather afraid that it is. I have ordered every assistance possible to be given to her.[9]

The wound was, indeed, to prove fatal. The accident had happened in a public house in the town. It is easy to see one of Cawdor's troopers bragging about his part in the affair, pulling out his gun and showing off before the assembled company – with, of course, disastrous results.

As for the prisoners, the damage they had caused and would continue to cause to churches like St Mary's could not be endured for long. Captain Longcroft, the Regulating Captain, managed to lay his hands on four brigs. These, he declared, would settle their hash.

The prisoners were marched off towards Milford and there they were put on the ships. For some strange reason the ships did not sail at once but sat there in the Haven with the disgruntled Frenchmen kicking their heels on board. As late as 1808 Thomas Noot, Ensign and Surgeon to the Fishguard Fencibles, wrote to the secretary of war requesting payment for treatment he had given to the prisoners while they were lying on the four brigs. Quite why he had waited over ten years to submit his claim is a matter of conjecture.

It was not just the prisoners that Noot was claiming for. The Fishguard Fencibles had been charged with guarding them and apparently several of them caught fever. For anyone who had seen conditions on board the ships it was hardly surprising. Conditions on the brigs closely resembled those on the prison hulks with some of the Frenchmen forced to lie on wet ballast.[10]

At the end of March 1797 four more ships were obtained. A total of 1,118 prisoners were now spread out between the eight vessels and then sailed out of the Haven and around the coast to Portsmouth. What awaited them, of course, were the infamous prison hulks. Apart from a handful who had been too unwell to travel and a group of approximately 400 left behind in Haverfordwest, that marked the end of the county's involvement with the French soldiers.

Sick and ill prisoners were becoming the bane of Lord Cawdor's life at this time. On 28 March Captain Longcroft informed him that: 'The prisoners getting very sickly, we have been absolutely obliged to send 126 of them to the Naval Hospital at Barne Lake.'[11]

Barne Lake was an inlet off the Cleddau River, directly opposite Pembroke Ferry where Cawdor's forces had crossed the river on the first night of the crisis. Longcroft had acted humanely but, even so, several of the prisoners subsequently died and were buried in the graveyard at Burton, the nearest village to the hospital.

The 400 men left in Haverfordwest were also soon moved, this time to the notorious Golden Prison in the south of the county.

The gaol sat on the banks of Pembroke River, within the shadow of Pembroke Castle, and was famous in the county for its slackness and ill-discipline. The fabric and structure of the building was none too secure either and it is not surprising that a number of prisoners managed to escape its confines.

The story of their escape is fascinating and has been told many times. Indeed, it seems that no telling of the invasion story is complete without some mention of the escape and of the romantic threads that weave through it.

There are a number of versions of the tale, so many in fact that it is hard to know where truth begins and fantasy ends. There was certainly an escape and the fundamentals of the legend remain consistent, whoever is telling it. The bare bones of the story are as follows: two of the French officers imprisoned at Pembroke became romantically involved with two local girls, Anne Beach and Eleanor Martin. The two Frenchmen are named by the writer John Kinross as a lieutenant, the former Marquis de Saint Armand (sometimes spelled Amans), and a grenadier sergeant by the name of Roux.[12] Interestingly, the Duke of Rutland makes no mention of their names when writing in his journal although he does make great play of the escape story.

With the help of the two Welsh women a tunnel was dug under the walls of the prison. Some versions of the story have Anne Beach and Eleanor Martin providing digging implements and then carrying away the soil from the diggings in the buckets they had used to bring in food for the prisoners. With the date for the escape set for early July, twenty-five Frenchmen waited their moment and then went down the tunnel and out of the prison.[13]

Accompanied by Anne and Eleanor, they made their way to Pembroke Quay below the castle and there boarded a small yacht, appropriately enough one owned by Lord Cawdor. They then sailed down Pembroke River and were soon in the broader expanses of Milford Haven. From there the open sea beckoned.

Off Linney Head the escapees fell in with a large merchant vessel which they duly captured by pretending to be shipwrecked sailors. They transferred to the larger vessel and Cawdor's yacht was cast adrift. She was, eventually, wrecked on the coast, some broken spars and bits of her rigging being all that remained of the tiny vessel.

A few days later the escaping Frenchmen, guided by the helmsman from the merchant vessel, reached St Malo. In due course the two girls married their lovers, Armand and Anne Beach even returning to Wales during the Peace of Amiens in 1802 and opening a tavern in Merthyr Tydfil.[14] When war broke out again the pair disappeared from Wales and were never heard of again.

It is the stuff of historical fiction – but then, so is much of the story of the landing. St Armand and Anne Beach were certainly an item. How they met has never been made clear but presumably the first meetings took place when the Frenchman was walking the streets of Haverfordwest and Pembroke while on parole.

St Armand and his colleagues were lucky; they had found freedom. The rest of the prisoners continued to kick their heels in gaol. But the escape had been the last straw for the Pembrokeshire authorities who now wanted nothing more than to be rid of their recalcitrant guests. News that they were to be removed from the county and taken to Portsmouth was received with mixed emotions by the prisoners.

Some, knowing the conditions they would shortly encounter on the prison ships, were worried and concerned. Others, eager for a change of scene, laughed and danced their way out of the Golden Prison. They were marched to the Haven, escorted by the Pembroke Fencibles and the Castlemartin Yeomanry, and put on board transport vessels. Their journey to the prison hulks of the south coast was short and after a few months they were sent back to France.

The arrival of these ruffians in their native land was not something that was greeted with universal acclaim, however:

> In October 1797 there were loud complaints from Cherbourg when one hundred and fourteen of them arrived as part of an exchange of four thousand prisoners to secure the release of the celebrated British frigate Captain Sir William Sidney Smith who had been imprisoned in Paris. Although the people of Cherbourg had no alternative but to accept their unwelcome guests, they speedily locked them up in the forts of the district.[15]

By a strange – and some would say, not undeserving – quirk of fate, these convict soldiers of the Legion Noire had ended up in exactly the same situation as they had left many months before. And there they sat, sorrier and more travel stained but certainly no wiser.

Chapter 17

The British, Too

For the British participants in the landing and its aftermath it was also time to move on – although many of them were unable to forget the momentous events in which they had been involved and were happy to tell and retell the story of those dramatic days for the rest of their lives. People like the Fencible Private H.L. Williams, even Lieutenant Colonel Knox, wrote and published their accounts of the invasion but they were in the minority. Talking about things in the pub or on the street corner was one thing; putting recollections down on the printed page was something different altogether.

In the main the ordinary men and women, people who had been involved in the events either as part-time soldiers or simply as observers, soon resumed their normal occupations. After all they were just sailors and farmers, shopkeepers and washerwomen, not men and women of substance. They had to work to survive.

Some, like Jemima Nicholas, achieved fame and, possibly, even financial reward. Whether she actually received her government pension is unclear and several historians have suggested that her money was appropriated by the local vicar rather than arriving at her door. At this time and distance it is hard to know where the truth lies.

Lord Cawdor was much praised for his part in the affair. He had conducted himself with great courage, with dignity and with a fair degree of talent and skill. He was not a professional soldier but he had proved himself to be a leader of considerable ability. At a meeting of the Nobility, Gentlemen, Clergy and Freeholders of the county, a meeting

convened and run by Lord Milford, on 18 March 1797, Cawdor's part
in the affair was formally acknowledged:

> It is resolved … that the thanks of this Meeting are
> particularly due and be given to the Right Honourable Lord
> Cawdor, for his spirited and decisive Conduct in leading
> the forces delegated to his Charge by the Lord Lieutenant,
> into the presence of the Enemy, through which, under the
> Protection of the Almighty, the Enemy felt the necessity
> of laying down their Arms and of surrendering themselves
> Prisoners to the Force of a Brave and determined People.[1]

The language is flowery and shows the pomposity, even the defensiveness
of Lord Milford – after all, he was the man who should have been
there marching towards Fishguard at the head of the troops, not Lord
Cawdor. And there is no mention of the vacillating and indecisive series
of heart changes that had marred the early part of the campaign. It is,
nevertheless, a handsome acknowledgement of Cawdor's contribution
to the British victory.

Lord Cawdor continued to command the Castlemartin Yeomanry,
albeit without further dramatic events like the invasion ever presenting
themselves again. The Yeomanry that he played such a large part in
creating retains the prestige of possessing the only Battle Honour to
'be held by any unit of the British Army for facing an enemy within
the British Isles'.[2]

Cawdor relinquished command of the Yeomanry at the time of the
Peace of Amiens and was succeeded in command by his great friend
and companion in arms Joseph Adams. By this time there was a second
Castlemartin Troop under the command of Lord Cawdor's brother,
Matthew Campbell. Cawdor himself continued to run his estates with
compassion and concern, the model of a good landowner and country
squire. He died at Bath on 1 June 1821 and was succeeded by his son
who was made Earl Cawdor of Castlemartin in 1827.

John Colby held command of the Pembrokeshire Militia, despite
his growing reticence and disillusionment, until 1800. He would have

preferred concentrating on matters of business and commerce but fate had always decreed otherwise for this eminently practical and sensible man.

Apart from his actions during the French invasion, his service record included a brief spell in Ireland in the summer and autumn of 1799. In July 1803 he was appointed Major in the Pembrokeshire Corps of Yeomanry Cavalry, rising to command of the Regiment in 1805. By 1807 he was High Sheriff of the county and died in 1823, leaving a wife, five sons and three daughters.

Of the others little is known. Thomas Nesbitt, whose conduct during the campaign had been exemplary, went on to serve as commissary for the county of Pembrokeshire and never did take the boat to Ireland – the sole reason for him being in Fishguard in the first place. He conducted the Duke of Rutland on a tour of the invasion area and was able to point out many of the important sites that the Duke might otherwise have missed.

Major Bowen, commander of the Newport section of the Fishguard Fencibles, succeeded Thomas Knox as head of the local defence volunteers while Captain Edwardes, Colby's companion for his night ride to the fort, later became the 2nd Lord Kensington. He was, briefly, an MP for Haverfordwest.

Longcroft, the Regulating Captain, was much praised for his part in the affair and during the follow up. He achieved the rank of Post Captain before dying at his home in Ceredigion in 1812. His two naval colleagues, Lieutenants Dobbin and Hopkins of the Customs Service, had also conducted themselves with diplomacy and honour and were well praised for their actions. As recognition for their part in the French defeat they were both presented with handsome ceremonial swords by the Customs Board.[3]

* * *

That, of course, left Lieutenant Colonel Thomas Knox and for him the future was neither so pleasant nor so prosperous. To begin with things did not start out that way.

As might have been expected the French defeat and surrender were at first met with liberal praise for anyone who had in any way been involved. Knox received his share. A royal message of congratulations was sent by George III to Knox and all of the commanders. The Duke of Portland had received a report from Knox on 24 February, at the very moment of the French surrender, and he now replied that the king was totally satisfied with the conduct of the Fencibles.[4]

Lord Milford, in the same Resolution that had been so fulsome in its praise of Lord Cawdor, had not forgotten Thomas Knox. Praising Cawdor was Resolution Number One of the meeting. Colby was featured in number two. The third finding was for Knox: 'The thanks of the meeting should be given to Lieutenant Colonel Knox who led the Fishguard and Newport Fencible Infantry.'[5]

Compared to the lavish praise for Cawdor and Colby that single sentence might seem a trifle understated, but Knox was well enough pleased. Certainly, at this stage, there was no indication of the troubles that lay ahead.

Once the prisoners had been placed on Longcroft's barges in Milford Haven, it fell to Knox to escort General Rooke around the invasion sites. There had been a rumour that 3,000 French muskets had been hidden on the Pencaer Peninsula, waiting to be collected by rebels and traitors. Knox was able to show Rooke that this was decidedly untrue and for this he received a letter of commendation from the general.

So far so good – but storm clouds were gathering. One evening a row erupted between Knox and Lord Cawdor. It was over a simple enough thing: sentries having been removed from the Haverfordwest lodgings of Colonel Knox. The young man felt slighted, felt that he and his position were being denigrated. It all passed off easily enough but it showed that there was no love lost between Cawdor and Knox and that it would take very little to create a major incident.

Duties over, Knox was back home at Minwere Lodge when he received news that a certain Major Williamson was coming to investigate serious charges that had been levelled against him. Knox was in the dark and had no idea what could be wrong.

It soon transpired that the charges were indictments of his leadership and personal courage. They had been levelled by Charles Hassall, the dismissed steward of Knox's father. Hassall had encountered the Fencibles during their retreat from Fishguard but, at the time, Knox had paid the man little attention. With hindsight it is easy to see that Hassall's charges were little more than an attempt at revenge on a family that he felt had treated him unfairly. At the time, however, they were treated seriously by the military authorities.

Hassall had sent a letter to a barrister by the name of MacNamara, telling him about what he considered cowardly behaviour on the part of Knox, behaviour that had put the whole country in jeopardy. MacNamara, supposedly incensed by Hassall's report then quoted the comments in a letter he sent to the Duke of York, commander in chief of the British Army.

Hassall, it seemed, was incensed at the decision to retreat from Fishguard. He was also particularly angry at Knox ordering the cannon in Fishguard Fort to be spiked. All of the officers and men, he said, were appalled by such cowardice, they had told him that when they met on the road from Fishguard. Hassall wrote that when he had met Knox and the retreating Fencibles he had tried to persuade their commander to return to what was now an undefended town: 'But the young gentleman thought it more prudent to provide for the safety of himself and abandon the town and neighbourhood to their fear and their fates.'[6]

The vindictiveness of Hassall shines through his comments. He was a writer and agriculturalist of some note but he was also a spiteful man with a short and violent temper. He had even fought a duel against General Picton – later killed at Waterloo – and as far as he was concerned the Knox family were fair game. In his letter, Hassall quoted many people who held similar views to him, including Gwynne Vaughan, Governor of Fishguard Fort.

Major Williamson soon arrived to begin his investigations. Knox was interviewed as were Gwynne Vaughan, Thomas Nesbitt and the Woolwich gunners who had refused to spike the cannon. In the wake of the investigation, Lord Milford – somewhat shamefacedly, it must be admitted – had no option but to ask Knox for his resignation.

Before Knox could reply, matters went up another notch. General Rooke received a letter that both shocked and appalled him:

Haverfordwest, 15 April 1797

Sir: We are conscious it is unnecessary to trouble you with assurances of our Loyalty and zeal for the State or Attachment to the interests to the County of Pembroke. We acknowledge with gratitude your attention to us when in Wales and feel highly honoured by the approbation you bestowed on our conduct. Anxious that no serious inconvenience might unexpectedly arise in this part of your District by the want of officers for the provincial Corps, at a moment their services may be required, we think it is our Duty to apprize you that the regard we feel due to our own Reputations as Officers must force us into the painful Necessity of resigning the Commissions we have at present the Honour to hold rather than under any circumstances risk our characters by acting under command of Lieutenant Colonel Knox whose ignorance of his Duty and want of judgement must be known to you.

We have the honour to be

With the sincerest regard

Your most Humble Servants.[7]

Rambling and sycophantic as it may have been, the letter was signed by no fewer than eighteen officers, including Lord Cawdor, Captain Ackland, Joseph Adams and Thomas Ridgway. Interestingly, Colonel Colby did not append his signature to the 'round robin' and remained one of the few senior officers of the time to give Knox his support. The young man, he believed, had acted out of poor judgement rather than cowardice.

Perhaps Colby remembered his midnight ride and the tremulous excitement of his meeting with Knox at Fishguard Fort. If he really did advise Knox to retreat – as Knox repeatedly claimed – he could not, in all honesty, now condemn him for cowardice. It may have been the wrong decision but Knox was, at that time, using what all military commanders were expected to use – individual judgement.

Cawdor was undoubtedly the driving force behind the letter to General Rooke. His was by far the most significant of the eighteen names on the document and his clashes with Knox, both during and after the campaign, were well known. Cawdor was, however, a man of honour and if he did instigate the deputation he must have believed that it was a necessary act. In light of that judgement the letter should be taken at face value and regarded as an indication of how people felt about Lieutenant Colonel Thomas Knox.

Williamson continued to hear evidence and Knox, desperate to clear his name, demanded an official court martial. His request was refused. Before any decision could be reached, however, General Rooke suddenly received a communication from the Duke of York's military secretary informing him that the Duke was more than satisfied with the conduct of Colonel Knox and that matters should now be allowed to rest.

If royal approval was behind young Knox, the man himself was bitterly hurt and dissatisfied. His reputation, he felt, had been sullied and he continued the fight to clear his name. Even so, in May he resigned his commission and the very next day wrote to Lord Cawdor asking to see a copy of the letter that he and his friends had sent to General Rooke. Cawdor's reply was immediate. He could, he declared:

> Feel no difficulty in stating the reasons that decided me to resign my commission, rather than risk my character as an officer by serving under your command, viz, my conviction of your inexperience and ignorance of your duty, joined to want of judgement. But I cannot transmit to you a copy of the letter you allude to with the signatures, without the permission of the officers whose names are affixed to it.
>
> I am, Sir, Your obedient humble servant, Cawdor.[8]

It was an honest but, to Knox, a bitter and a hurtful reply, the last straw to an ego already badly damaged by the charges laid against him by Hassall. He had, he felt, just one recourse left to him – he challenged Cawdor to a duel.

As he had been challenged, Cawdor had the right to decide on weapons and on a time and a place for the duel. He chose the turnpike road between Williamston and the ferry point on the north side of the Cleddau. Knox and Cawdor duly met at noon on a hot Wednesday, 27 May 1797. The result of the duel – if it ever took place – is unknown.

In his diary entry for the day Cawdor records, laconically enough: 'Wednesday 24 May 1797. A very fine day; after breakfast rode to the ferry. Met Jos there, and Mr Knox and Colonel Vaughan, near the Williamston Road. Rode home, back by half past one.'[9]

Joseph Adams had acted as Cawdor's second; Colonel Vaughan seems to have been pressed into service with Knox. In all probability the duel was never fought. Cawdor was not one to spill blood unnecessarily and the chances are that he talked Knox out of any intemperate action. If it did take place, neither party seems to have been hurt and honour would have been satisfied by a quick crossing of blades or a pair of pistol shots into the air.

As Knox had resigned his commission, Cawdor and the other officers withdrew their resignations and continued to serve to the best of their abilities. Knox, on the other hand, continued to fulminate over what had happened to him. Nobody seemed inclined to listen, not the War Office or any government department – and certainly not the people of Pembrokeshire.

The Knox family had never been popular in the county, despite the undoubted brilliance of Knox Snr. They were always regarded as in-comers and upstarts. Their haughty behaviour and arrogant demeanour merely confirmed this opinion.

Knox wrote a book in an attempt to clear his name, sticking rigidly to his opinion that Colby had advised him to retreat if he thought it necessary. The messenger from the Haverfordwest Committee, William Fortune, confirmed this in Knox's book, as did many of the Fencible officers. He was, they wrote, a man of honour who had acted at all times with integrity and spirit.[10]

It made little or no difference. He was never reinstated to his post and strangely, his accusers – Hassall and MacNamara in particular – were never charged with libel or called to account in any way. At the end of the day they seem to have got away, scot free, with casting aspersions on a man who may have displayed want of judgement, but who was certainly not a coward.

The final years of Thomas Knox were unhappy and unstable. He was angry and bitter at the way he had been treated, but his real regret and the real driving force behind his anger was that he could not forgive himself for retreating from Fishguard and leaving the town open to the French. The fact that they never came was immaterial. They could have, that was the point. Cawdor or Colby would not have retreated or withdrawn. Knox knew that and the knowledge haunted him for the rest of his life.

He became convinced that he was an unrecognised military genius, telling everyone who would listen. He became estranged from his family and embroiled in a tempestuous love affair with a girl called Catherine Phillips. The affair ruined him financially and in 1825 he died in poverty in London, a sad end for a man who had once held the fate and the future of the whole country in his weak and pliable hands. He was 56 years old.[11]

The dust slowly settled on the French landing at Fishguard. As those who had been involved died off, all that was left was legend, a strange mishmash of truth and fiction. Above all there remained, and still remains, a huge sense of regret. What could have been, what might have happened, seems to be the overall feeling, from both sides.

Perhaps the fate of Thomas Knox, like that of William Tate, sums up the rather ludicrous invasion. From the activities of the Legion Noire to the battle that never took place, the whole affair seems somehow tinged with an air of sadness. It hangs across the invasion site, across the whole of the Peninsula, like one of the winter mists that still descend every now and then on the coast. There have been sorrier wars, no doubt, but never one so doomed to failure.

Conclusion

The 1797 French landing on the Pencaer Peninsula outside Fishguard was the last time that any invader's foot has ever rested on the soil of mainland Britain. It is now well over 200 years since the French arrived and caused utter panic in the area. The invaders tarried briefly and then disappeared before they could cause any lasting damage but the story still retains the power to enthral, entertain and intrigue.

No matter how you look at it – an enterprise always doomed to disaster, a chance to instil republican values and ideals in what was, then, a truly conservative nation, a forlorn hope or a way to rid France of unwanted soldiers and convicts – it is the characters that stand out.

There is an old adage that any good novel, any good story, should contain the three p's – place, people, problem. It does not take long for the reader to discover that the last invasion has them all. The setting is wonderful, the problem is obvious but, in particular, it is a story that is replete with fascinating people.

From Tate and the Irish officers to Cawdor and Jemima Nicholas, the story of the landings is full of memorable figures, some great, others minor, but all of them worthy of mention and remembrance. Apart from their value as story characters they are a reminder that we are all of us making history every day of our lives. The labourers and fishermen who made up the Fishguard Fencibles did not realise that they were making history in 1797 but that was what they were doing every time they assembled for parade and throughout the three or four days of the invasion scare.

The effects of the invasion were many and varied but the one that we all too often forget is the simplest – no other invader has ever succeeded, even for the briefest of moments, in landing armed forces in Britain. This truly was the Last Invasion of Britain.

In some respects it is an epitaph that Tate and Hoche would not have liked, mainly because the invasion did not succeed. In other ways they would probably have been proud. Tate and his men did at least get ashore. And they certainly caused confusion and mayhem in the ranks of British rule. So maybe it was not all bad.

The question has to be asked – who exactly were the victors? Certainly not the British Army. No regular troops were involved from beginning to end. The answer is simple – Lord Cawdor and the local people of Pembrokeshire. Whether they served as Fencibles or Volunteers, whether they just tagged along to do what they could, it was the solidarity and the strength of ordinary people – ordinary women in many cases – that brought victory to the defenders.

As part of the celebrations for the centenary of the invasion, held in Fishguard in 1897, the Reverend J. Symonds composed a Centenary march. It may not have been great poetry but it certainly caught the mood of the time and, with hindsight, with the mood of 1797 as well:

> Gladsome day, we now remember
>
> Thus the great events of old,
>
> When our fathers were delivered
>
> From the French invader bold.
>
> Hardy local men and women
>
> Joined with Cawdor's noble name
>
> Under heaven's kindly leading
>
> Were the means to quench the flame.

Lord Cawdor and the local people was a strange but powerful alliance, a coming together of high and low born. It was something to which the French had no answer and it still retains the ability to send the hairs on the back of your neck shooting suddenly upwards.

The centenary of the invasion was celebrated in 1897. Among other things there were parades and concerts, a march out to the headland – with 'Jemima' suitably prominent – and the unveiling of a memorial stone high on the top of Careg Wastad Point. The rest of Britain may have forgotten the landings but the people of Fishguard certainly had not.

The centre point of the bicentenary celebrations in 1997 was the unveiling of The Last Invasion Tapestry. It was a mammoth production, created by various groups from the area, and one that was as significant as the famous Bayeux Tapestry. As one local wit put it: 'Down here we have our own Bayeux Tapestry – the Over by 'ere Tapestry.' Only in Pembrokeshire! The massive embroidery tapestry is now on display at the Fishguard Library.

The tapestry is a beautiful, even magnificent piece of work. It takes a distinctly traditional view of the events of 1797. There is nothing wrong with that; it is all part of the legend, the wonderful creation of one of the best-loved tales of Wales.

Adversity invariably brings out the best in people, creating leaders and fighters who might otherwise remain silent and unheard. The examples are obvious; Churchill in the Second World War, Lloyd George in the First; Nelson and Alfred the Great; Queen Elizabeth at the time of the Armada. Lord Cawdor and the people of Pembrokeshire fit easily into that collection of heroes.

Notes

Introduction

1. William Hoste in *The Faber Book or Reportage*, London, Page 253
2. Oliver Tearle *Britain By the Book*, John Murray, 2017, Page 204

Chapter One

1. F. Jones *The Harries of Tregwynt*, privately printed, 1946, Page 10
2. Doreen Yarwood *The English Home*, Batsford, 1979, Page 130
3. H.L. Williams *An Authentic Account of the Invasion by French Troops*, privately printed, 1842, Page 6
4. Commander E.H. Stuart Jones *The Last Invasion of Britain*, University of Wales Press, 1947, Page 85
5. Ibid, Page 85

Chapter Two

1. Simon Schama *Citizens*, Penguin, Page 51-55
2. Simon Schama *Citizens*, Penguin, Page 55
3. https://en.wikipedia.org/wiki/Girondins
4. Lucy de la Tour du Pin *Memoirs of Madame de la Tour du Pin*, McCall, Page 139
5. David Williams *A History of Modern Wales*, John Murray, Page 171
6. William Wordsworth *The Prelude*, Methuen, Page 5
7. Ibid, Page 5
8. John Kinross *Fishguard Fiasco*, H.G. Walters, Page 11

9.   Frank McLynn *Invasion*, Routledge and Kegan Paul, Page 81
10. Oliver Tearle, Ibid, Page 203
11. BBC History Revealed, March 2018, Page 103

Chapter Three

1.   https://en.wikipedia. org/wiki/Carnot
2.   wiki://en.wikipedia.org/wiki/WolfeTone
3.   W.T.W. Tone 'The Life of Wolfe Tone', 2 Vol1, Page 52
4.   Simon Schama, Ibid, page 467
5.   Stuart Jones, Ibid, Page 16-17
6.   J.E. Thomas *Britain's Last Invasion*, Tempus, Page 54
7.   Frank McLynn, Ibid, Page 85
8.   John Kinross, Ibid, page 30

Chapter Four

1.   Herbert W. Richmond *The Invasion of Britain*, Methuen, Page 38
2.   Frank McLynn, Ibid, Page 86
3.   E. Desbriere 'Project et tentatives du debarquement dansles Iles Britaniquen,' Vol 1, Page 213
4.   Frank McLynn, Ibid, page 88
5.   *Daily Journal of Lord Cawdor*, Cawdor Papers
6.   Stuart Jones, Ibid, page 20
7.   Herbert W. Richmond, Ibid, page 39

Chapter Five

1.   Stuart Jones, Ibid, Page 7
2.   E. Desbriere, Ibid, page 239
3.   Pamela Horn *History of the French Invasion of Fishguard 1797*, Preseli Printers, Page 3
4.   Stuart Jones, Ibid, page 53
5.   J.E. Thomas, Ibid, Page 58
6.   Pamela Horn, Ibid, page 3

7. E. Desbriere, Ibid, page 239
8. Phil Carradice *The Last Invasion of Britain*, Appendix, Village Publishing, Page 147
9. https://en.wikipedia.org/wiki/battleofFishguard
10. https://en.wikipedia.org/wiki/LegionNoire
11. Organisation of the Legion Noire, Cawdor Papers, 223/12
12. Deposition of Nicholas Tyrell, Public Record Office, PC1/37, A114
13. Deposition of Barry St Leger, Public record Office, PC1/37, A114
14. Hoche's Instruction for Colonel Tate, quoted in Phil Carradice (Appendix), Ibid
15. David Salmon 'The French Invasion of Pembrokeshire,' article, West Wales Historical Society magazine 1936

Chapter Six

1. Stuart Jones, Ibid, Page 66
2. Deposition of Nicholas Tyrell, Ibid
3. H.L. Williams, Ibid, Page 9 and Ferrar Fenton *Landing of the French at Fishguard*, Page 67
4. Lord Milford, quoted in 'Sarah Farley's Bristol Journal, 24 March 1797.'
5. John Kinross, Ibid, Page 45
6. Deposition of Robert Morrison, Public Record Office, PC1/37, A114
7. Letter to the Duke of Portland, Cawdor Papers, 223/19
8. Deposition of Barry St Leger, Ibid
9. Deposition of Nicholas Tyrell, Ibid
10. Reverend Daniel Rowlands *The Fishguard Invasion by the French*, Fisher Unwin, Page 47-48
11. Ibid, page 47-48
12. H.L. Williams, Ibid, Page 5
13. Reverend J.W. Maurice 'History of the French Invasion of Fishguard in 1797', *The Echo*, Page 2

14. Pamela Horn *The Building of Fishguard Fort*, Preseli Printers, Page 2
15. John Kinross, Ibid, page 24–24
16. Pamela Horn, Ibid, page 5
17. John Kinross, Ibid, page 26

Chapter Seven

1. Details of the Establishment of the Fishguard Fencibles, Cawdor Papers, 223/17
2. Cawdor's Account of the Invasion, (unpublished) Cawdor Papers 223/8
3. Thomas Roscoe *Wanderings and Excursions in South Wales*, Henry G. Bohn, Page 200
4. Ferrar Fenton, Ibid, page 4
5. Deposition of Barry St Leger, Ibid
6. Stuart Jones, Ibid, Page 183
7. Deposition of Barry St Leger, Ibid
8. Ibid
9. John Kinross, Ibid, Page 48
10. Bill Fowler *The French Invasion at Fishguard*, Dyfed Education Department, Page 11
11. Lieutenant Colonel Howell 'The Pembroke Yeomanry,' article in *The Pembrokeshire Historian*, 1966

Chapter Eight

1. Letter from Gwynne Vaughan to the Duke of Portland, PRO HO 42/40
2. Ibid
3. Stuart Jones, Ibid, Page 71
4. Ferrar Fenton, Ibid, Page 64
5. Lieutenant Colonel Howells, Ibid, Page 75
6. John Kinross, Ibid, Page 18
7. Jane Austen *Pride and Prejudice*, Pan Books, Page 53

8. Fowler, Ibid, Page 11
9. John Whiting *Penny for a Song*, Heinemann, Page 26
10. Phil Carradice, Ibid (Appendix) Page 137
11. A Return of Forces under Lord Cawdor, Cawdor Papers, 223/16
12. Ibid
13. Lieutenant Colonel Howell, Ibid, Page 75
14. Ibid, Page 76

Chapter Nine

1. Stuart Jones, Ibid, Page 100-101
2. Ibid, Page 24
3. J.E. Thomas, Ibid, Page 44
4. Stuart Jones, Ibid, Page 25
5. Ibid, Page 31 and Page 40

Chapter Ten

1. Letter from Lord Milford, Cawdor Papers, 223/19
2. Phil Carradice *A Town Built to Build Ships*, Accent, Page 28
3. Letter, Cawdor Papers, 223/18
4. Ibid, 223/18
5. Fishguard Arts Society, web page
6. Stuart Jones, Ibid, Page 92-93
7. Letter to the Duke of Portland, Cawdor Papers, 223/11
8. Account of Expenses Incurred, Cawdor Papers, 223/11
9. Letter to the Duke of Portland, Cawdor Papers, 223/19
10. Peter Thomas *Politics in Eighteenth Century Wales*, UWP, Page 8
11. Resolution of General Meeting, Cawdor Papers, 223/1
12. Letter to John Vaughan, Cawdor Papers, 223/19
13. Return of Forces, Cawdor Papers, 223/16
14. Parish Register, Roch, 22 February 1797, Pembrokeshire Record Office
15. Deposition of William Fortune, No 23

Chapter Eleven

1. Sarah Farley's Bristol Journal (then published as a booklet), Carmarthen Records Office
2. Rudyard Kipling 'A Smuggler's Song', Kingfisher, London
3. Stuart Jones, Ibid, Page 102-103
4. Bella Bathurst *The Lighthouse Stevensons*, Harper, Page 24-25
5. H.L. Williams, Ibid, Page 9
6. Phil Carradice, Ibid, Page 139
7. Film *The Man Who Shot Liberty Valance*.
8. H.L. Williams, Ibid, Page 22
9. Stuart Jones, Ibid, Page 84
10. Ibid, Page 84
11. Lord Cawdor's Account (unpublished), Cawdor Papers, 223/18
12. Roch Parish register, Ibid
13. John Kinross, Ibid, Page 55
14. Quoted in Kinross, Ibid, Page 56

Chapter Twelve

1. Log entry by Castagnier, quoted in Salmon, Ibid, Page 140
2. Pamela Horn, Ibid, Page 10
3. Ibid, page 10
4. E. Hermitage Day, article in *The Treasury*, undated
5. Rev J.W. Maurice, Ibid, Page 3
6. Deposition of Barry St Leger, Ibid
7. Deposition of Robert Morrison, Ibid
8. Ibid
9. Ibid
10. H.L. Williams, Ibid, Page 236
11. Ferrar Fenton, Ibid, Page 66

Chapter Thirteen

1. Sarah Farley's Bristol Journal, 4 March 1797
2. H.L. Williams, Ibid, Page 20

3. Ibid, Page 20
4. David Salmon, Ibid, 1937
5. Sarah Farley's Bristol Journal, Ibid
6. Quoted in John Kinross, Ibid
7. H.V. Morton *In Search of Wales*, Methuen, Page 197-198
8. Diary/Journal of Lord Cawdor, Cawdor Papers
9. Frank McLynn, Ibid, Page 89
10. Stuart Jones, Ibid, Page 115
11. H.L. Williams, Ibid, Page 20-21

Chapter Fourteen

1. Letter from Lord Cawdor to the Duke of Portland, Cawdor Papers, 2123/19
2. John Kinross, Ibid, Page 62
3. Letter, Cawdor to Duke of Portland, Cawdor Papers, 223/19
4. Rev. J.W. Maurice, Ibid, Page 21
5. Ferrar Fenton, Ibid, page 66
6. Ibid, page 66
7. Rev. Daniel Rowlands, Ibid, Page 133
8. H.L. Williams, Ibid, Page 42
9. Letter to the *Times*, Cawdor Papers, 223/19
10. Letter to Mrs Mary Harry, Cawdor Papers. 223/19
11. 'A Native', article in *Chambers Journal of Popular Literature*, issue NO 315
12. John Kinross, Ibid, Page 49
13. Despatch to the Admiralty from Sir H.B. Neale, PRO (Admiralty)
14. Ibid
15. Ibid
16. Phil Carradice, Ibid, Page 75

Chapter Fifteen

1. Thomas Roscoe, Ibid, Page 201
2. David Williams, Ibid, page 174

3. John Kinross, Ibid, page 88-89
4. Ferrar Fenton, Ibid, Page 62
5. Letter from Colonel Colby to Home Office, quoted in Stuart Jones, Page 152-153
6. John Kinross, Ibid, page 98-99
7. Stuart Jones, Ibid, page 211
8. Pamela Horn, Ibid, Page 17
9. Stuart Jones, Ibid, Page 212
10. The Duke of Rutland 'Journal of a Tour through North and South Wales and the Isle of Man,' privately printed, Page 161-162
11. Ferrar Fenton, Ibid, Page 10
12. Phil Carradice, Ibid, Page 58
13. Philip MacDougall *Royal Dockyards*, Barracuda Books, Page 20
14. Pamela Horn, Ibid, page 18
15. David Williams, Ibid, Page 174-175
16. Stuart Jones, Ibid, Page 167
17. Quoted in Stuart Jones, Page 176
18. *Gentleman's Magazine*, Page 576

Chapter Sixteen

1. Letter from Carmarthen Mayor, PRO HC42
2. Letter, Cawdor to his wife, quoted in Pellatt-Elkington *The Last Invasion of Wales*
3. Ibid
4. Deposition of Morrison and Tyrell, PRO
5. W. Branch-Johnson *The English prison Hulks*, Christopher Johnson, Page 51
6. Ibid, age 84-85
7. Stuart Jones, Ibid, Page 138
8. John Kinross, Ibid, Page 100
9. Letter from Captain the Hon. Edwardes, Cawdor Papers, no number given
10. Letter from Dr Noot, quoted in Stuart Jones

11. Letter from Captain Longcroft, Cawdor Papers 223/2

12. John Kinross, Ibid, Page 91

13. H.L. Williams, Ibid, Page 27

14. Ibid, Page 28

15. Pamela Horn, Ibid, Page 15

Chapter Seventeen

1. Resolution of Pembrokeshire Gentry, Cawdor Papers, 223/1

2. Lieutenant Colonel Howell, Ibid. Page 76

3. Stuart Jones, Ibid, Page 109 and Page 255

4. Thomas Knox 'Some Account of the Proceedings,' Page 80

5. Resolution of Pembrokeshire Gentry, Ibid, Cawdor Papers 223/1

6. Quoted in Kinross, Page 78

7. Copy of letter to General Rooke, Cawdor Papers, 223/19

8. Letter from Lord Cawdor, quoted in David Salmon, Ibid, Page 179

9. Diary/Journal of Lord Cawdor, entry for 24 May 1797

10. Thomas Knox, Ibid, Page 81-82

11. Stuart Jones, Ibid, Page 203

Bibliography

Primary Sources

The Cawdor Papers is a huge reserve of material, held at the Carm-arthen Record Office, containing letters to and from Lord Cawdor, Lord Milford, the Duke of Portland and so on. It also contains lists of forces and stores at the time of the invasion, press cuttings, and depositions and so on. The collection is vast and goes beyond the French invasion but it remains essential reading for anyone with an interest in the events of February 1798. The following records have been particularly useful in writing this book:

1. Resolution of a General Meeting of the Nobility, Gentlemen, Clergy and Freeholders of the County of Pembroke, 1797. 223/1
2. Letter from Lord Milford to the Commanding Officer of the Yeomanry Cavalry, Pembroke, 22 February 1797. 223/19
3. Letter to John Vaughan, Esq, 23 February 1797. 223/19
4. Letter from Lord Cawdor to the Duke of Portland, 5 March 1797. 223/19
5. Account of the French Landing by Lord Cawdor, unpublished paper. 223/8
6. Details of the Establishment of His Majesty's Corps of Fishguard Volunteers, commanded by Lt Col Thomas Knox, 28 February 1797. 223/17
7. Return of Military Stores at the Commissary's different store houses in Haverfordwest, 3 July 1797. 223/7
8. Copy of letter to Mary Harry, servant, 27 February 1797. 223/19
9. Return of French Killed near Fishguard from 22 February to 25 February 1797. 223/10

10. A Return of Forces under the Command of the Rt Hon. Lord Cawdor that Marched to Fishguard against the Enemy, 23 February 1797. 223/16

11. Copy of letter from Alexander Ridgway to The Times. 223/19

12. Minutes of Meeting Convened by the Lord Lieutenant of the County of Pembroke, London 19 April 1794. 223/6

13. Organisation of the Legion Noire. 223/12

14. Letter from Captain Longcroft to Lord Cawdor, 28 March 1797. 223/18

15. A Return of Sea Officers who put themselves under the Command of Captain E Longcroft and Joined Lord Cawdor when he went out to meet the Enemy. 223/18

16. Return by Captain Longcroft of the Vessels in Milford Haven with French Prisoners on Board, 27 March 1797. 223/2

17. Account of the expenses incurred by Pembroke Ferry for carrying troops and soldiers during the French invasion, 27 April 1797. 223/11

There are many other documents at the Carmarthen Record Office, perhaps not technically part of the Cawdor Papers but closely linked and therefore equally as important. Chief among these additional papers or documents is The Daily Journal of Lord Cawdor for 1797. Cawdor was an inveterate writer in his diary and this book gives a valuable insight into the life and times of the landed gentry at the end of the nineteenth century.

The Parish Register for Roch, kept on a daily basis by a diligent and interested vicar, also gives interesting detail of the invasion period. It is held in the Pembrokeshire Record Office in Haverfordwest.

Other primary source material is available from the Public Records Office at Kew. Of particular interest are:-

The Deposition of Barry St Leger, PC1/37, A114

The Deposition of Robert Morrison, PC1/A114

The Deposition of Nicholas Tyrell, PC1/A114 (with addendum by Nathaniel Oliver)

Letter from Gwynne Vaughan, Governor of Fishguard Fort, to the Duke of Portland, 42/40

Despatch from Sir HB Neale to the Admiralty

Letter from the Mayor of Carmarthen to the Duke of Portland regarding the French stay in the town

Published Books

Anon 'History of the French Invasion of Pembrokeshire,' reprinted as booklet from the Journal of Welsh Biographical Society, 1937

Austen, Jane, *Pride and Prejudice* Pan, London, 1967 (originally published 1813)

Branch-Johnson, W., *The English Prison Hulks* Christopher Johnson, London, 1957

Bathurst, Bella, *The Lighthouse Stevensons* Harper, London, 2005

Carey, John, (ed.) *The Faber Book of Reportage* Faber, London, 1987 – article by William Hoste

Carradice, Phil, *The Last Invasion* Village Publishing, Pontypool, 1992 *A Town Built to Build Ships* Accent, Cardiff, 2014

de la Tour du Pin, Lucy, *The Memoirs of Madame de la Tour du Pin* McCall, New York, 1971

Desbriere, E., *Project et tentatives du debarquement dansles isles Britaniquen* unknown publisher, quoted in Stuart Jones, 1902

Fenton, Ferrar, *Landing of the French at Fishguard* Pembrokeshire Antiquities, Haverfordwest, 1897

Fowler, Bill, *The French Invasion at Fishguard* Dyfed Education Department, Undated, Haverfordwest

Horn, Pamela, *The Building of Fishguard Fort* Preseli Printers, Fishguard, 1982

Horn, Pamela, *History of the French Invasion of Fishguard* Preseli Printers, Fishguard, 1980

John, Brian, *Ports and Harbours of Pembrokeshire* Pembrokeshire Handbooks, Fishguard, 1974

Jones, F, *The Harries of Tregwynt* reprinted as booklet from the Translations of the Honourable Society of Cymmrodorian, 1946

Jones, Commander E.H. Stuart, *The Last Invasion of Britain* University of Wales Press, Cardiff, 1947

Kinross, John, *Fishguard Fiasco* H.G. Walters, Tenby, 1974

Knox, Thomas, *Some Account of the Proceedings that Took Place on the Landing of the French near Fishguard on 22 February 1797* London, 1800

MacDougall, Philip, *Royal Dockyards* Shire Publications, Buckinghamshire, 1989

Maurice, Rev. J.W., 'History of the French Invasion of Fishguard in 1797', the Echo, Fishguard, 1896

McLynn, Frank and Kegan, Paul, *Invasion* Routledge, London, 1987

Morton, H.V., *In Search of Wales* Methuen, London, 1947

Pellatt-Elkington, F., *The Last Invasion of Wales* undated, unattributed

Richmond, Admiral Sir Herbert W., *The Invasion of Britain* Methuen, London, 1941

Roscoe, Thomas, *Wanderings and Excursions to South Wales* Bohn, London, 1854

Rowlands, Rev. Daniel, *The Fishguard Invasion by the French in 1797* T. Fisher Unwin, London, 1892

Rutland, Duke of, 'Journal of a Tour through North and South Wales and the Isle of Man,' privately printed, London, 1805

Salmon, David, 'The French Invasion of Pembrokeshire in 1797,' reprinted as booklet from The West Wales Historical Records, Vol 1V, 1930

Schama, Simon, *Citizens* Penguin, London, 1989

Tearle, Oliver, *Britain by the Book* John Murray, London, 2017

Thomas, J.E., *Britain's Last Invasion* Tempus, Stroud, 2007

Thomas, Peter, *Politics in Eighteenth Century Wales* University of Wales Press, Cardiff, 1998

Tone, W.T.W., 'The Life of Theobald Wolfe Tone, Vol 1,' no publisher listed, London

Whiting, John, *A Penny for a Song* Heinemann, London, 1964

Williams, David, *A History of Modern Wales* John Murray, London, 1950

Williams, H.L., *An Authentic Account of the Invasion by French Troops (Under the command of General Tate) on Careg Wastad Point near Fishguard* Haverfordwest, 1842

Yarwood, Doreen, *The English Home* Batsford, London, 1979

Poetry Anthologies

Rosen, Michael, (ed.) *The Kingfisher Book of Children's Poetry* Kingfisher, London, 1989

Evans, Sir Ifor, (ed.) *Selections from Wordsworth* Methuen, London, 1966

Websites

https://en.wikipedia.org/wiki/Battleof Fishguard

https://en.wikipedia.org/wiki/LegionNoire

www.fishguardartssociety.org.uk

https://en.wikipedia.org/wiki/Girondins

Articles

BBC History Magazine, January to December 2017

BBC History revealed, March 2018

Sarah Farley's *Bristol Journal*, 4 March 1798

The Gentleman's Magazine February 1797

Chambers Journal of Popular Literature – article called 'How the French Fared at Fishguard' by A Native – 14 January 1860, Issue No 315

The Pembrokeshire Historian – article by Lieutenant Colonel R.L. Howell called 'The Pembrokeshire Yeomanry,' Issue No 2, 1966

The Treasury – article by E. Hermitage Day called 'The Last Invasion,' undated (copy held in Pembrokeshire County Library, Haverfordwest)

Acknowledgements

Thanks are due to many people who helped, in one way or another, with the making of this book. In particular a huge net of gratitude must go to the following:

The ordinary men and women of Fishguard who did not despair when the French landed in 1797 and who would never have dreamed that their stories would still be told over 200 years later – without them this book would not have been possible.

Village Publishing, now long defunct, who took the chance on the original book which ran through several editions and has now culminated (in a vastly different form) in this new volume.

Roger MacCallum, as ever, presiding genius and master of technology – without you, Rog, nothing would have happened.

The staff of Carmarthen and Pembrokeshire Records Offices. Also the staff of the County Library in Haverfordwest.

My son Andrew who drew several illustrations and maps to make the visual side of the book very different indeed.

Trudy, who stood by my shoulder and watched: God bless you sweetheart, remember when you first typed up the original MS? This one is in your memory.

About the Author

Phil Carradice is a poet, novelist and historian. He has written many books, the most recent being *The Cuban Missile Crisis* and *The Bay of Pigs*, both for Pen and Sword, and *The Call Up* (Fonthill). His most recent novel is *Stargazers* (Accent Press). He is a renowned teacher of creative writing and a regular broadcaster on BBC radio and television.

Index